T0120983

NEW BEGINNINGS
RESPONDING TO THE CALL
"EFFECTIVE STRATEGIES THAT PROMOTE AND PROVOKE
DAILY MANIFESTATION!!!"

"**A** *Highly Effective Training Manual Designed With Successful Strategies Directly Focused On Teaching People How to Developed a Winning Mindset,*"

DR. LAWRENCE V. BOLAR

authorHOUSE®

AuthorHouse™
1663 Liberty Drive
Bloomington, IN 47403
www.authorhouse.com
Phone: 1 (800) 839-8640

© 2018 Dr. Lawrence V. Bolar. All rights reserved.

No part of this book may be reproduced, stored in a retrieval system, or transmitted by any means without the written permission of the author.

Published by AuthorHouse 03/20/2018

ISBN: 978-1-5462-3294-0 (sc)
ISBN: 978-1-5462-3293-3 (e)

Library of Congress Control Number: 2018903125

Print information available on the last page.

Any people depicted in stock imagery provided by Getty Images are models, and such images are being used for illustrative purposes only. Certain stock imagery © Getty Images.

This book is printed on acid-free paper.

Because of the dynamic nature of the Internet, any web addresses or links contained in this book may have changed since publication and may no longer be valid. The views expressed in this work are solely those of the author and do not necessarily reflect the views of the publisher, and the publisher hereby disclaims any responsibility for them.

English Standard Version (ESV)
The Holy Bible, English Standard Version. ESV® Text Edition: 2016. Copyright © 2001 by Crossway Bibles, a publishing ministry of Good News Publishers.

New Living Translation (NLT)
Holy Bible, New Living Translation, copyright © 1996, 2004, 2015 by Tyndale House Foundation. Used by permission of Tyndale House Publishers, Inc., Carol Stream, Illinois 60188. All rights reserved.

New International Version (NIV)
Holy Bible, New International Version®, NIV® Copyright ©1973, 1978, 1984, 2011 by Biblica, Inc.® Used by permission. All rights reserved worldwide.

Amplified Bible (AMP)
Copyright © 2015 by The Lockman Foundation, La Habra, CA 90631. All rights reserved.

New King James Version (NKJV)
Scripture taken from the New King James Version®. Copyright © 1982 by Thomas Nelson. Used by permission. All rights reserved.

King James Version (KJV)
Scriptures were taken from The King James Version of The Bible - Public Domain.

Contents

The Declaration of Life:

Life is a journey and on every journey there is a need for declarations:

This book is my testament that God is real; and He is faithful and bound by His word. The creation of this book was neither by my might nor by my power. This book was created, and inspired by God, that I might be a living testimony of His grace, kindness, and overwhelming love as a living witness for all to marvel at his miraculous power. I declare by the promises of God that this book will glorify His Name and bring edification to His kingdom.

I strongly believe that the words on these pages will introduce, expose, enlighten, educate and teach every reader about His will as it pertains to their life.

You will be blessed by reading this book from the front cover, to the back cover and you shall be blessed by sharing its content. I am blessed in knowing that this book is based on God's Holy and Devine Word. I am blessed because of my convent relationship with God's Holy Word. This is New Beginnings: Responding to the call!

Created By: Dr. Lawrence V. Bolar

Motivational moment by the Author

<u>In everyone's life, there is a strong need for encouragement
to not just survive our journey in life but to thrive!</u>

Aborting your dreams

How does one pursue success in today's corrupt society with
its impenetrable systems and impoverished mindset? Fighting
off the stain of fame or wealth, prosperity over salvation it
starts with a new beginning by responding to the call.

Pursuing The Power in you starts by taking ownership! As an
educator, author, and coach my primary mission is to create and
inspire every individual to unleash the untapped, unthinkable
talent that God created in them. Too many people have tapped out,
kicked out and aborted their dreams. No matter whom you are
or what stage in life you discover yourself in today, without God
your thoughts are killing you! Why because our minds are often
our worst enemy. If you want to make changes in life you have
to push yourself as if your life and legacy depends solely on it!

Laziness destroys dreams, indecision is a thief in life, and
procrastination is enemy number one. So fighting while at
war with the mind is not an option! You have to fight with
everything in you to keep your brain from sabotaging your
dreams. What you are and what you become depends on you!
Take total control over your destiny and believe that you can be
more than a conqueror in all that you do with the confidence
that no weapon formed against or created by you will prosper!

Created By: Dr. Lawrence V. Bolar

"Every moment is a fresh beginning." —*T.S. Eliot*

"The first step towards getting somewhere is to decide you're not going to stay where you are." —*John Pierpont "J.P." Morgan*

"A journey of a thousand miles begins with a single step." —*Lao Tzu*

"Every new beginning comes from some other beginning's end." —*Seneca*

Quotes by Dr. Lawrence Bolar

<u>Creating quotes to live by are essential to finding balance in life!</u>

1. There isn't always enough time in a day to march to the beat of another's man drum but if you will let him know how he sounds, you have helped him along his way.

2. Fatherhood isn't always filled with moments of excitement but its priceless principles should be earmarked as footprints molded in the sands of his children's mind to be embraced and embedded for generations to come.

3. Life doesn't just pass us by it disappears at the twinkling of an eye, so grab hold to your dreams and live each day as if it was your last.

4. My life is not all about gains or losses or who I can become but about whom can I carry along the way.

5. When you realize that your dreams that you have been dreaming are no longer a dream but a reality just know it was God

6. When life's struggles begin to tug away at your heart and you can't see your way through just remember it's just a test from God to strengthen you.

7. Knowing who you are makes it easier to become who you where destined to be.

8. A saved life is a life filled with unlimited expectations.

9. There is no fear in the unknown for the unknown only exist in him who does not know Him who created it.

10. God see's in me what I cannot see in myself, for I am truly blinded by the limits I have created in me.

11. No obstacles known to man can keep me out of God's hands for I am not my own I was created purposefully in his image for his glory.

12. Be not angry for what you have been through for it has created in you a fire forged by heavens hands.

13. The champion in me was forged out of pain that my purpose in life could be substained.

14. Who could have imagined that my birth would be so tragic and my end be so amazing.

15. The confidence is not in what I can see but, in what I can believe.

16. Listening and then responding can determine a successful outcome

17. Learning the why, can often prevent the what from being understood.

18. Who then can stop a dream driven by my flesh other than the spirit of God?

19. It's impossible to become what you do not believe.

20. Love understands The Who not the why.

21. My beginning does not determine my end.

22. What I cannot believe will never be achieved.

Isaiah 43:18-19 English Standard Versions (ESV)
[18] "Remember not the former things, nor consider the things of old. [19] Behold, I am doing a new thing; now it springs forth, do you not perceive it? I will make a way in the wilderness and rivers in the desert.

Chapter 1

New Beginnings

What has life been like for you? Have you ever found yourself being or feeling less than what you were created to be? Have you watch things in life over take you with or without your knowledge? Have you witnessed things working out for others but not for you? Have you ever imagined dying before your time or burying your love ones before their expected time? Are you always feeling anxious or fearful over large and small situations or circumstances? All of these questions and so many more you can expect to be answered in New Beginnings, Responding to the call!

Thank you for selecting this book as it will bear fruit into your life. I know that there are millions of books out there that are phenomenal to read. This book on the other hand is that and so much more. New Beginnings has been forged, created and designed to challenge and redirect your way of thinking, responding to the impact and effecting change to your life forever. This book has been carved out especially for you. The things you will have the opportunity to read, experience, learn about, study and explore will cause positive change in your life, I declare it.

I believe by faith that each reader who wholeheartedly studies, embrace, and take this book into their spirit, it will further bring them new life and establish multiple New Beginnings. I also recommend that as often as you read this book, read it out loud in your home or your car. The power of your voice combined with these words and scriptures possess a much greater impact than you will ever know. Remember this one thing that in your voice there is an unimaginable power to create or destroy.

> **2 Corinthians 5:17 English Standard Version (ESV)**
> [17] Therefore, if anyone is in Christ, he is a new creation.[a] The old has passed away; behold, the new has come.

I know that New Beginnings has the power and the capacity to change lives immediately! The impact of this body of work will be manifested in each reader's life and the life of their loved ones daily. Please allow, New Beginnings to intoxicate your spirit with its powerful scriptures and declarations, so that life for you will never be the same. I hope you have ready every poem, quote, motivational moment, and textbox statement. If not, stop now, go back and start reading them, take them because they are designed just for you. Ok, I think you're ready now, let's delve into this journey. Ready, set, begin.

The dawn of each new day provides the opportunity to start fresh and new daily. No matter what obstacles yesterday presented or what new challenges that tomorrow will bring, trust, faith and belief consist of a triangulation of power that will propel mountains to be removed, destroyed, and cast away with one decision. I know this kind of sound unreal, and unbelievable, in fact it sounds like a bunch of hype until you decide to act, move or make a decision. Once a decision has been made, the manifestation immediately happens. Yes, the power immediately manifest with one simple decision after the next. This decision must begin with the renewing of your mind from all of the disastrous undertakings that each day brings.

There are literally thousands of things fighting your attention, seeking to distract you from your focus and purpose in life. These things come in very subtle ways not to cause any major attention but to serve as major distractions. One major example, is daydreaming, focusing on things that don't really matter or beneficial to your ultimate purpose and goal in life. The mind can really be a terrible distraction when and if it's not brought under subjection. The undertakings of the mind can cause mass destruction that has the capacity to last a life time thereby causing collateral damage. The undertakings are that of:

1. **Disappointment**

2. **Traumatic experiences**

3. **Tragedies**

4. **Deaths**

5. **Mishaps**

6. **The inability to recognize who is in control.**

> **Jeremiah 29:11 English Standard Version (ESV)**
> [11] For I know the plans I have for you, declares the LORD, plans for welfare[a] and not for evil, to give you a future and a hope.

Today, all that can be put behind you with one decision and that decision is to take full control and kindly hand it over to God who cares for you and me immensely. Testing is a part of life. No life is without test. The difference is are you willing to release your control over to Him who is the blessed control of life. Once you are confident of who is in control of your life and the power you possess, life as you once knew it becomes different and your purpose will be achieved. Will you allow today to be your New Beginning?

New Beginnings is a book designed for the new convert or a beginner in the gospel of Jesus Christ, also known as the good news. I guarantee this book will take you places you never imagined. The book is designed specifically for new converts but it reminds veteran converts of their existing authority in Christ while reminding them of their decision to follow Christ. This authority is like no other. In order to receive this message, you must open up your heart, spirit, and mind. I'm confident that after reading and studying this book along with your Bible, life as you once knew it will be no more.

First Strategy: The Power of an open mindset:

The power of an open mind can catapult you into seeing and understanding the unknown! Opening our minds allows us to expose the world to the greatness God has given to us. Often, we discover some of the greatest minds, talents, gifts and ideas are lying in the grave never to be produced or manifested. The question you must ask yourself is, will I leave this world without ever becoming who I was meant to become?

Our minds are closed in reference to how we see ourselves. What you think about yourself matters much more than you can even imagine. In fact, what you think about yourself out weighs what your friends, family, or organization think about you. The opinion of others are a great source of information, however, it's just their opinion of who they think you are. I have discovered that a large group of people rarely open their minds up to what they can see. Do you know who you were created to be? I am created in the image of God and so were you too. The next time you look in the mirror remember whose image and likeness you were created in. Going to the mirror should never be the same again. See yourself as different and unique.

I can't change my past but I can begin to change my future and my destiny. In fact, it's either now or never because our dreams cannot wait. Look at how long we have already held ourselves up from reaching our goals and divine purpose. This sense of urgency comes with knowing the life I live is not my own, but every individual tied to or connect to me. There are people in line for you to impact them in a way that will change their life. Today is not the day to delay; you must not delay, because you were born on purpose, and with a purpose.

My question still remains the same, how do you see yourself? Do you see yourself as limited or without limitations? How you see your self is very important, if I fight for my limitations I

> **Ephesians 4:22-24 English Standard Version (ESV)**
> 22 to put off your old self,[a] which belongs to your former manner of life and is corrupt through deceitful desires, 23 and to be renewed in the spirit of your minds, 24 and to put on the new self, created after the likeness of God in true righteousness and holiness.

may just get to keep them. I know that is an oxymoron, but it's a truth that we must all suffer to overcome. The world is filled with thousands of daily choices, therefore life is all about choice. Humanistic ally is how we think and grow based on trial and error. I must choose to delete my limitations in order to grow without limits. Growing should be done daily as a living vessel for we are lifelong learners. Dealing with our fears or weaknesses allows us to grow stronger. A growth in our mindset teaches us how to conquer our fears.

The challenge people face often is the fight to keep their limitations and fears and this can be dangerous. This reinforces a double mindset. People operating in this mindset often find themselves unstable in all of their ways. A physiological prison without walls or chains, in essence controls the mind and the heart. Control of the mind and heart is unparalleled. Controlling these two key components can be disastrous. Prison in the contrast does not entail the physical prison, it's mental!

STOP, LISTEN & BREATH:

This section is designed for salient points and takes a ways from what you just read!

Notes:

_____

_____

_____

_____

_____

_____

_____

> **Philippians 4:6-7** "Don't worry about anything; instead pray about everything. Tell God what you need, and thank Him for all he has done. Then you will experience God's peace, which exceeds anything we can understand. His peace will guard your hearts and minds as you live in Christ Jesus."

Chapter 2

Responding to the call

Responding to the call is not nearly as difficult or as challenging as our fleshy emotions lead us to believe. Our emotions and feelings are full of tricks and deception which are inspired by the enemy of our souls. The enemy to our souls is no other than the master trickster, Satan himself. The reasons the tricks of the enemy are so effective in our lives is because our flesh collaborates with the enemy and when this happens all hell breaks loose. I find that a lot of people Christian people in general don't realize that their own flesh conspires against them.

I use this term all hell breaks loose because every demon in hell rejoices. The demonic forces count this as a victory against us even though he plays a very insignificant part or role in the success. The reason demons count this as a victory is because they believe that they have won the battle. In fact, for all intense purposes it appears that he is always going to win the war. The reason for the celebration is because although it appears as if you are going on with life as usual without one single bump in the road or hiccup, however it's not so. Although, the enemy is wise and strategic in his dealing with us, but he is not alpha and omega. The enemy can only go off of his past experiences and believe that the traps he has set are final. These delays do not deny the call that God has in our lives. God through the power of the Holy Spirit is a gentleman and will never enforce or impose anything on man, therefore giving man the will power to decide.

Oftentimes, decisions are made based on what feels good and what doesn't feel good without giving a whole lot of meaningful thought behind the consequences of our actions. The actions that affect us and our family, love ones and the generations to come thereafter. Major decisions about our lives are made without consulting God, his Holy word, leaders, or counselors in Christ Jesus. The baffling thing is that a major decision has been made about the course of your life, the next generation and generations to come. The sad truth is you are completely unaware of it; in fact you are oblivious to what has happened in your life. The true victory for the enemy is because you are completely dumbfounded of what has just taken place or the mere impact it has on your entire family. The enemy knows that while you're in a state of haze, blurredness, or simple incoherent state of being. God's purpose and plan for your life has being brought to a halt and rendered powerless, useless, and has no penetration power for you to win or power to help others win! You are in a state where you're walking around alive but yet dead. The kingdom of God suffers mightily at your hand and you are silent, unable to protect, defend, warn or aid the building of the kingdom of God. You often count yourself out of the race and you don't even know why. You often think by avoiding or denying the truth that you're aiding when you are really destroying yourself through self-condemnation. Don't allow self condemnation become your best friend. New beginnings is available for you today, just respond to the call and life for you my friend will never ever be the same. You are not a victim; you are a Victor in Christ Jesus!

My mission is to persuade you by any means necessary to know and respond to your call that it may be well with your soul. Shifting our focus on God creates a manifestation for New Beginnings and this brings about a divine changes. I strongly believe that there is a supernatural call on all of our lives! The question is how you will personally respond to God's call in your life. The bizarre thing is although you may not have a desire to respond appropriately to the call, your lack of a response is a response! You may run, duck, or hide from the call but your life will reflect your response of the call.

Recently a very old, yet extremely important friend of mine reentered my life after nearly twenty-five years of no real contact. You know this had to be the divine purpose of God. I have searched high and low for this brother and he has been hidden from me all these years. I looked for him so long and so hard that I had finally taped out when I received an email from him. Talking about the importance of a new beginning, who would have thought that God would allow this to happen after twenty-five years? Really? I am so amazed, at God's handy work and timing. God is all powerful and all knowing, when I looked I could not find him but God's perfect time is awesome.

The friendship was pure and honest that we would work out together and hangout in the campus library on a regular basis laughing and just having a wonderful time. No real cares in the world, just too young men whose only real common interest was to be successful college students and men. We would often have heavy debates over just about anything in life. The awesome thing was that we were to people who rarely disagreed and never fell out about anything. We mutually admired one another's work out habits and developed our friendship primarily in the gym. In fact, now that I think of it, that's where it all began, that's where we met and spent a great deal of time working out and chatting. I was most impressed with his strength and power to lift extremely heavy weights with such skill and ease. These were some of my greatest workouts still today. I have yet to find a work out partner of his caliber. I remember attempting to persuade him about the goodness of Jesus and the importance of being saved. I would strategically mention things about Sunday school and how important it was to learn about God.

During most of our workouts, I would often share with him the goodness of God that I was experiencing and he would listen but wasn't very fazed by anything I said or so I thought. This would last throughout our friendship. I wasn't sure if anything I said penetrated his system or if the seeds I was attempting to plant was falling on good ground or not! I just recently learned that although it appeared to me that the seeds were falling on rocky hard places and would not produce fruits I discovered that a harvest had begun. The scripture teaches us that some plant seeds, some water the seeds, but it's God who provides the increase.

This same friend shared with me his secrets of the road to great success and wealth; however, somewhere down the road all he obtained could not withstand his sudden health battle with an aneurysm. So what exactly is this? A brain (cerebral) aneurysm is a bulging, weak area in the wall of an artery that supplies blood to the brain. In most cases, a brain aneurysm causes no symptoms and goes unnoticed. In rare cases, the brain aneurysm ruptures, releasing blood into the skull and causing a stroke. Only God could have known such a thing. This is another reason to have a personal relationship with God. The word of God teaches us that warning comes before destruction and that nothing shall over take us unawares.

I have decided to include the detailed information about his experience because it was new to me and I felt it would be educational for each reader. When a brain aneurysm ruptures, the result is called a subarachnoid hemorrhage. Depending on the severity of the hemorrhage, brain damage or death may result. The most common location for brain aneurysms is in the network of blood vessels at the base of the brain called the circle of Willis. The power of God has a way of capturing our attention and placing us on our backs thereby leading us back on track, but as the great Les Brown says if you fall, fall on your back because if you can look up, then you can get up.

What causes a brain aneurysm?

A person may inherit the tendency to form aneurysms, or aneurysms may develop because of hardening and narrowing of the arteries (atherosclerosis) accompanied with aging. Some risk factors that can lead to brain aneurysms can be controlled, while others can't. The following risk factors may increase your risk for an aneurysm or, if you already have an aneurysm, may increase the risk of it getting ruptured:

- **Family history.** People who have a family history of brain aneurysms are more likely to have an aneurysm than those who don't.
- **Previous aneurysm.** People who have had a brain aneurysm are more likely to have another.
- **Gender.** Women are more likely to develop a brain aneurysm or suffer a subarachnoid hemorrhage.
- **Race.** African Americans are more likely than whites to have a subarachnoid hemorrhage.

- **High blood pressure.** The risk of subarachnoid hemorrhage is greater in people who have a history of high blood pressure.
- **Smoking.** In addition to being a cause of high blood pressure, the use of cigarettes may greatly increase the chances of a brain aneurysm rupturing.

I know reading this will galvanize someone to consult with their doctor and keep their health checked before for the Lord. All very important reasons as to why I included this very important information for your reading pleasures. The most important reason is because of the power of God supersedes anything even this ailment.

In getting back to New beginnings, I and this same friend of mine I mentioned earlier had a reunion and the connection was so divine. The connection continued with the fact that I'm delighted to report that after twenty-five years I received a strange email over the weekend 1/20/18 with the name of my long lost friend whom I had not heard from in many years. In receiving the email, I was shocked because I knew this name but I wasn't sure if it was the person I had search for vigorously over and over again for years with No real success. The emails didn't share enough information about him, rather they were just single lines just stating and to verify that he was who I thought that he was. No real enthusiasm from a person I knew to be very enthusiastic.

I was extremely excited but nervous because I wasn't totally sure if it was my friend or not and I really didn't want to be disappointed if it wasn't him. I emailed him my number in hopes that if this really was him that he would reach out to me. Sure enough he did, late on Sunday evening I received a strange call I didn't answer. The number was a Texas number and I was confident it was him. So, I quickly listened to the voice message something I rarely do immediately. The voice message only mentioned it was him and he stated his name.

I could vaguely here the voice but yet I knew the voice was his. I wasn't sure if I wanted to return the call back immediately or wait until morning. I asked Niki for her advice and she instantly said of course you should call him immediately, haven't you been looking for this guy for years with no success, what are you, a fake friend? My only rationale that I shared with her was that it was late; her response was well didn't he call you and it was late.

Based on this conversation, I was galvanized into action. I called him and we were caught up talking late into the night and now we have begun a New Beginning and I'm proud to say my friend has answered the call! Perhaps, one day I will share with you in more details, the only thing I can say is I am in awe of God and his love for us as his children. Only God can reconnect you with someone in his own unique fashion. Thank you God for reconnecting me with my friend for over 25 years. The connection has truly been an answer to prayer.

The call is simple, the call is easy! The reason I said that is because obedience can be the beginning of your life, or the end of your life! Responding to the call that God has in your life prevents you from guessing on how long to travel successfully along life's journeys. This doesn't mean you won't have challenges you must face but it does guarantee your success.

If you want to be successful in this life you must respond to the call that God has in your life!

Step1. Learn more about who God is by studying his Holy Word! Speak to God in prayer by sharing his word back unto him. No matter how smart you maybe God understands his word. The word says if any man lacks wisdom let him ask it of God. The Holy Scripture says to study is to show yourself approved rightly dividing the word of truth! This is the beginning of your communication with God. Studying his word and giving it back to him in prayer.

Step2. Consistently walk, live and conduct yourself in a manner worthy of the Lord by fully pleasing him and desiring to please him in all things, and bearing fruit in every good work. This consistently builds your faith in God and allows you to mature in the things of God. This step allows you to be delivered from your crooked and wicked ways that you may be open to love your enemy as yourself as God requires.

Step3. The reception of God's Holy Spirit and a never ending love gauge. A light that sits upon a hill that others may see and follow your light to God. These steps releases the darkness within us that connects us to our enemy, Satan the devil. In understanding God's truth, there is no fear in believing in Satan and his deceptions. However, take courage in knowing God is All Powerful and Supreme. For it is impossible those who have been once for all enlightened, who has consciously tasted the heavenly gift and have become sharers of the Holy Spirit (Hebrews 6:4)

Following these three steps will cause our lives to be great. Please continue to read that so you may continue to discover your purposes in life and your mission to complete God's call in your life and fulfill your assignment for kingdom building. One of the goals of this book is build your relationship with God so that your motives will be cleansed to do this most Holy work in Christ Jesus!

Chapter 3

The Journey

> **Philippians 1:6** I am sure of this, that He who started a good work in you will carry it on to completion until the day of Christ Jesus.

If you're reading this then you're no longer trying to decide if this is a book worthy of reading and purchasing. Let me reassure you of your answer to that question which engulfs you. This is one of the best books you will ever find. This book will unpack things you may not have ever believed, imagined or witness before in your life. There are things that happen in life and we have no answers for them. I believe this book will walk you through whatever challenge you may be facing in life and make you better than you where before you began reading it. I will outline and introduce you to the Holy savior that lives today and guides you in the direction that will change your entire life. The only thing I ask each reader to do is keep an open mind, and view God from your heart, mind and spirit. I believe if you do that then this book will captivate you from the beginning until the end.

I know your eager to jump right into reading but I would like to begin your reading with a few survey question and answers first.

1. Do you believe in your heart that Jesus Christ died for the sins of this world? _____!
2. Do you believe that Christ will return again and that you have the opportunity to live an eternal life with him? _____!
3. Are you willing to accept him as your personal savior and learn of him and follow his principals in life for the rest of your life? _____!

If the answer is yes to these simple questions then I would ask that you repeat and confess with your mouth open right now. "Lord Jesus, come into my heart right now, I accept you as Lord and Savior over my life." My friend if you truly believe what you have just confessed openly with your mouth and believe in your heart you are saved; now you must get into a bible believing church that will teach you how to follow Christ. God bless you and always know that this is the book for you. My goal is to teach you and provide you with some baseline information that will affect and change your life forever.

New Beginnings ultimate design is to introduce you to Christ, reacquaint you to Christ and to enhance your current relationship with Christ and take it to a new level with Him. I have discovered that sometimes depending on how you were raised or your individual expectation of who God is, who he is to you, and how you fit into the grand scheme of God's plan for your life varies greatly from one Christian believer to the other. This is why New Beginnings has been established, to create order and constant guidance to Christ.

I have met people who have no direction or purpose that leads or drives their life. Without vision people perish! No matter your age, gender or ethnicity, there is a need to know and understand your God given purpose in life. If one does not know who they are then they can never become who they were ultimately created to be. My question for you at this point is, do you know who you are, what's your purpose in life, and who where you created to be? If the answer for you my friend is that you do not know, then you are reading the right book! Take courage in this very important scripture in Mathew 6:33 it will explain your direction, enhance your prospects and ultimately shape your purpose in life.

1 Samuel 2:35 Unfolds Gods thoughts and Plans for our life

'Then I will raise up a faithful priest for Myself. He will do whatever is in My heart and mind. I will establish a lasting dynasty for him, and he will walk before My anointed one for all time.

We can clearly see that this matter is very personal for God. God takes his personal assignments to us very, very serious and there is neither room nor opportunity to deviate outside of God's plan for our lives and even when we try, the end results aren't in our favor similar to that of Jonah running away. Please familiarize or read the story of Jonah, its quite fascinating. What caused Jonah to even think that he has the capacity to run and hid from an Almighty God. In his defense, he had no clue to the amount of biblical information we have at our finger tips now. I would like to hope and believe that a modern day Jonah wouldn't think twice about running from God.

How does one begin to think of a place to hide that God cannot find. This vague and shallow idea only prolonged and caused grave discomfort to him. The chapter of I Samuel 2:35 speaks specifically of that of Eli, the Priest and his wicked sons. This is another very important story to read. The story of Eli and his sons provides a great outlook on how God views our responsibility to the purpose that he had ordained for our life. The story of Eli leads to death! God is very serious about what you are doing or what you are not doing concerning the building of his kingdom. For example, your desire to win souls, your desire to tell everyone about Him, your desire to study and learn of Him, your desire to open your mouths and give thanks, give adoration praise speak well of him. Who amongst us is void of being able to do these very things?

Spiritual blood line

Oftentimes we are defined and we define others by our bloodline or our families we were birthed into. These blood lines can and often dictates and determines our future before we are rebirth with a new beginning. In other words, if we are born into a family of weaklings, thieves, liars, gossips, murders, alcoholics, whoremongers and impoverishment. People often tag us with the things they identify our family members with. The enemy of our souls also takes these imaginations and promotes them in our minds without us ever recognizing what's happening to us.

James 1:8
[8]he is a double-minded man, unstable in all his ways.

For years, we go around with a defeated mindset always thinking less of ourselves or feeling like we cannot make it in life. What I think about myself is valuable and it is these thoughts that will either create a champion in me or a defeated mentality. Our minds are like computers, we download negative and defeated thoughts in our minds.

> **1Peter 5:8** Be sober-minded; be watchful. Your adversary the devil prowls around like a roaring lion, seeking someone to devour.

Colossians 3:2
Set your minds on things that are above, not on things that are on earth.
What are you expecting from God?

Mark 13:34 The level of Authority that the Believer has

It is like a man going on a journey, having left his house, and having given his servant's authority to handle each one of his work. And he commanded the doorkeeper that he should keep watch.

> **My appointment here was not by accident and neither was yours, but that of a divine spiritual purpose.**

There is a powerful anointing on the Spiritual appointment. There is a heavy drawing of God's Power here that will elevate you to reach your divine appointment.

1. Transform
2. Reconfigure
3. Establish your legacy in God through this sure and enduring house of God.

In order to be a sure house in God you have to

1. Know and be confident that you have been transformed

change, alter, convert, metamorphose, transfigure, transmute, mutate;
revolutionize, overhaul;
remodel, reshape, redo, reconstruct, rebuild, reorganize, rearrange, rework, renew, revamp, remake, retool;

The thing you should want most is God's kingdom and doing what God wants. Then all these other things you need will be given to you.

Question:

1. Have you figured out Gods purpose for being in a sure and enduring house?

2. Where is your authority?

Oftentimes people either don't realize or recognize their authority or either it's been on the shelf for so long that they don't know what to do with it or perhaps they lost it. Like Sampson, he took his authority for granted and he lost it.

Chapter 4

Seeing Beyond what you can see with your natural eyes

> **2 Kings 6:17**
> Then Elisha prayed and said, "O LORD, I pray, open his eyes that he may see "And the LORD opened the servant's eyes and he saw; and behold, the mountain was full of horses and chariots of fire all around Elisha.

We are living in a time where we face enormous attacks of the enemy but "no weapon formed against us shall prosper." The key thing to remember is, although weapons may form they cannot succeed with the mission of destruction. There is a ferocious war going on and some of us are simply oblivious and unaware of it and have no clue about the role they are created for. Some of us know but lack the authority it takes to operate in it. See even if you know and don't have the authority to walk in what God has designed for your life it's still rendered ineffective useless against Satan. Meaning we have power through God's Holy word and by the blood of Jesus Christ who died for us. The scriptures are very clear when it states, No weapon formed against us will prosper. The only fear the Christian has is the fear of the Lord.

Psalm 19:9 The fear of the LORD is pure, enduring forever. The decrees of the LORD are firm, and all of them are righteous.

There is power in walking in your authority

Some people right here, right now reading this feel like they have no authority! I'm willing to bet you have never stood up to the devil to confront him and say in the name of Jesus, take your hands off of my family and without having to ask someone to come and cast out the devil for them but as a born again believer you have the authority to do so. Everyone has faith, you have faith that the lights will come on when you flick the switch, and when you turn the door knob, you have faith that the door is going to open. Christians and non-Christians alike have that kind of faith. However, not everyone has faith in God.

The kind of faith the Bible talks about is centered on believing in God. Hebrews 11:6 says: "Without faith it is impossible to please God," because anyone who comes to Him must believe that He exists and that He rewards those who earnestly seek Him." Here, we see three elements of a faith that pleases God: (1) we must believe that He exists; (2) we must believe that He rewards; and (3) we must believe that He will reward us when we seek Him.

Faith Is

Hebrews 11:1 tells us, "being sure of what we hope for and certain of what we do not see." It is the confidence that things yet unseen will happen as God said they will. It involves accepting God's perspective as He reveals it in the Bible.

When there was nothing, God created everything. "By faith we understand that the universe was formed at God's command, so that what is seen was not made out of what was visible" (Hebrews 11:3). Colossians 1:16-17 builds on that same thought, letting us know that all things were created by Him and for Him, that He is before all things, and in Him all things hold together.

This is our God. Nothing is too difficult for Him to do. He is the all-powerful One who created the entire universe, yet He cares about you and will reward you when you earnestly seek Him and his righteousness. He holds the world and everything in it together, and He is willing and able to see you through any problem you will ever face.

Faith Goes Through

No one has the luxury of going through a problem-free life. The psalmist wrote, "A righteous man may have many troubles, but the Lord delivers him from them all" (Psalm 34:19). Just knowing that God's plan is to deliver you should make it a bit easier to have an enduring faith, one that holds on to God even in the time of trouble.

In Isaiah 43:1-2, God said, "Fear not", for I have redeemed you; I have summoned you by name; you are mine. When you pass through the waters, I will be with you; and when you pass through the rivers, they will not sweep over you. When you walk through the fire, you will not be burned; the flames will not set you ablaze."

All of this and more God has promised his children. There is a war waging on earth and we as the children of God must prepare for the battle. Our weapons are not carnal but spiritual. Therefore, we must study the word of God that we maybe skilled warriors rightly dividing the word of truth. The next few pages will focus on the importance of knowing who you are and where you stand in the army of the Lord. There is no greater way of knowing where you stand than being put to the test as true believers. Take courage in knowing that we are victorious in all things Christ Jesus.

What type of believer are you:

➤ What kind of believer are you when the enemy comes in like a flood?
➤ When adversity comes
➤ When your financially wiped out
➤ When health is challenged
➤ When all manner of evil is eating at your front door and attempting to take you over.
➤ Remember the prodigal son, we must come to our senses and recognize that in my father's house there is safety

11 Important things that every believer should know

1. The word of God gives me knowledge, provides direction, purpose, and guidance through and by studying the word of God.

2. My tongue activates my faith into existence. Calling things out, releasing angels to attack, bind up, loose up, and to set free.

3. The blood of Jesus seals and confirms the word of God toward my problems the very moment I release it, the blood of Jesus activates the authority in the Power of Jesus blood.

4. Know this, you have to walk it out by faith whether you visually see it or feel it (example the fig tree that Jesus spoke to and cursed).

5. When you have a sure house and an enduring house it should be in your walk, in your talk, and in your spirit. Your very presence has extreme power because of the Holy Spirit in you, brings torment to the enemy.

6. Learn how to combat the enemy when he brings up your past, say my past is no more! Jesus forgave me and tossed it in the sea of forgetfulness. Then, bring up Satan's past and let him know that you know what really happened on the cross! Oh by the way, let him know that you read in revelations what happens in his future. Learn to be sure bold and confident with Satan when he tries to talk trash to you, let him know that you already know his future and his expected end because you jumped to the back of the book of revelations and discover that in the end he loose.

7. He's like the big bad wolf he will huff and puff and blow your house down, but you stand flat footed and sure on the promises of God. Speak to the enemy and say to the enemy

not by the power and might of my Lord and Savior Jesus Christ we have that kind of authority.

8. Brothers and sisters, I know you have challenges with your faith at times but just hold on to Gods unchanging hand. A good faith building story is in 1 kings 18:44 finally the seventh time, his servant told him, "I saw a little cloud about the size of a man's hand rising from the sea." Then Elijah shouted, "Hurry to Ahab and tell him, 'Climb into your chariot and go back home. If you don't hurry, the rain will stop you!'"

9. Remember God's goodness and His greatness in your life and stop talking about what the enemy is doing, it glorifies him and we don't ever want to do that.

10. Find a body or group of believers to worship and fellowship with. Strong groups or body of believes are a great opportunity to talk about what God has done and this will create a room for us to look back at the hand of God.

11. Don't lose the awe of what God has done.

Believers often forget the Powerful things God has done in their life!

Example: The miracle of the five loaves of bread and Jesus walking on water that same day they had forgotten about

Matthew 14:13-21 Jesus Feeds the Five Thousand

13 When Jesus heard what had happened, he withdrew by boat privately to a solitary place. Hearing of this, the crowds followed him on foot from the towns. 14 When Jesus landed and saw a large crowd, he had compassion on them and healed their sick.

15 As evening approached, the disciples came to him and said, "This is a remote place, and it's already getting late. Send the crowds away, so they can go to the villages and buy themselves some food."

16 Jesus replied, "They do not need to go away. You give them something to eat."

17 "We have here only five loaves of bread and two fish," they answered.

18 "Bring them here to me," he said. 19 And he directed the people to sit down on the grass... Taking the five loaves and the two fish and looking up to heaven, he gave thanks and broke the loaves. Then he gave them to the disciples, and the disciples gave them to the people. 20 They all ate and were satisfied, and the disciples picked up twelve basketfuls of broken pieces that were left over. 21 The number of those who ate was about five thousand men, besides women and children.

Jesus Walks on the Water

22 Immediately Jesus made the disciples get into the boat and go on ahead of Him to the other side, while he dismissed the crowd.23 After he had dismissed them, he went up on a mountainside by himself to pray. Later that night, he was there alone, 24 and the boat was already a considerable distance from land, buffeted by the waves because the wind was against it.

25 Shortly before dawn Jesus went out to them, walking on the lake. 26 When the disciples saw Him walking on the lake, they were terrified. "It's a ghost," they said, and cried out in fear.

27 But Jesus immediately said to them: "Take courage! Don't be afraid."

28 "Lord, if it's you," Peter replied, "tell me to come to you on the water."

29 "Come," He said.

Then Peter got down out of the boat, walked on the water and came toward Jesus. 30 But when he saw the wind, he was afraid and, beginning to sink, cried out, "Lord, save me!"

31 Immediately Jesus reached out his hand and caught him. "You of little faith," He said, "why did you doubt?"

32 And when they climbed into the boat, the wind died down. 33 Then those who were in the boat worshiped him, saying, "Truly you are the Son of God."

34 When they had crossed over, they landed at Gennesaret. 35 And when the men of that place recognized Jesus, they sent word to all the surrounding country. People brought all their sick to him 36 and begged him to let the sick just touch the edge of his cloak, and all who touched it were healed.

STOP, LISTEN & BREATH:

This section is designed for salient points and takes a ways from what you just read!

Notes:

_____

_____

_____

_____

_____

_____

Chapter 5

What Do you really know about what you know

> **2 Corinthians 3:16**
> but whenever a person turns to the Lord, the veil is taken away

Do I know it all? No certainly not. I simply want to take you on a journey and teach you about a savior who can save your body and your soul, that you may find comfort in knowing where you will spend your eternal life after death. The book is based on the Holy Scriptures as provided by the bible. The expressed intent is to prove the average every day person or anyone who has a desire to have a better understanding and relationship with Christ Jesus. I know this book will help you in some capacity in your life's journey.

Often times, I have looked for practical self-help books with no success. I believe this book will be so much more than some self-help or motivational book. I know it will impact lives for centuries to come. I talk to a lot of people in all walks of life in my personal and profession line of work, and in the schools or in the community. I recognized that a lot of people are lost and they are in need of a savior. Another major reason for writing this book is to redirect my attention and my audience attention back to my original roots. My original roots begins and end with my Savior, Christ Jesus. My life in Christ has provided me the opportunity to forge ahead and be the individual that I desire to be despite my odds.

Jesus Christ is the very bedrock of all my writing whether I make it a plan or infuse it into my writings. Since my goal is to write and publish every year, the Lord has laid upon my heart this will power to write a book that is strictly about edifying the body of Christ Jesus. This book will be book number eight for me. I write with the intent to build and encourage all men. My life has been one of great adversity and of great blessings. So as a result, I wanted to write this book for others to envision, comprehend and experience my life through their lens that their individual life or calling can be more productive. Let me begin by saying I don't know everything and at this stage in life I am nobody's pastor or spiritual leader, rather I am simple, a man who benefits from being in a relationship with Christ Jesus. All of my success now and in the future has come from my relationship in Christ Jesus.

Last but certainly not the least, I have decided to team with other followers of Christ to hear their testimonies of Christ. You can find their testimonies in the second to last chapter of this book. Some are pastor's teachers and followers. Most importantly, they have decided to follow Jesus and their lives will indicate their strengths, their favorite scripts and persuades you to follow after God everyday of your life with expectancy, understanding and purpose.

> **Proverbs 3:7-8** "Don't be impressed with your own wisdom. Instead, fear the Lord and turn away from evil. Then you will have healing for your body and strength for your bones.

STOP, LISTEN & BREATH:

This section is designed for salient points and takes a ways from what you just read!

Notes:

_____

_____

_____

_____

_____

_____

_____

_____

_____

_____

_____

Chapter 6

Strategies of Faith that Work towards building your spiritual development

> **Hebrews 11:6**
> And without faith it is impossible to please him, for whoever would draw near to God must believe that he exists and that he rewards those who seek him

I believe that the church today has grossly underestimated the importance of faith. No believer can fight the good fight of faith without faith. A believer who has lost his faith is doomed and the enemy will certainly destroy their every step. The child of God must always meditate on God's word in his or her walk of faith. It is essential in every Christian walk to enact faith in all that we do. Faith goes beyond just salvation; it is the doorway that enables God to work both in and through us. Faith helps us grow, can change lives, moves mountains, and allows miracles to happen.

How important is faith? It takes faith to even believe in Christ; it takes faith to believe that what God says is always right and true; and it also takes faith to trust and walk in that each and every day that comes and passes by. However, if your faith doesn't continue to grow in your relationship with Christ, you won't have the faith to see God's Kingdom come not only in your life, but in the lives of those around you.

Whatever faith you have inside of you will determine the outcome of the faith level you'll have for God at work and all around you. If you don't have faith for God to move, there's a good chance you won't be looking for anything to take place.

Here are some additional scripture to
put in your spiritual tool box.

Mathew 17:20
20 He replied, "Because you have so little faith. Truly I tell you,
if you have faith as small as a mustard seed, you can say to this
mountain, 'Move from here to there,' and it will move. Nothing will
be impossible for you."

Hebrews 11:6
6 But without faith it is impossible to please him: for he that cometh
to God must believe that he is, and that he is a rewarder of them
that diligently seek him.

James 2:14-26
Faith Without Works Is Dead
14 What *does it* profit, my brethren, if someone says he has faith but
does not have works? Can faith save him? 15 If a brother or sister
is naked and destitute of daily food,16 and one of you says to them,
"Depart in peace, be warmed and filled," but you do not give them
the things which are needed for the body, what *does it* profit? 17
Thus also faith by itself, if it does not have works, is dead.
18 But someone will say, "You have faith, and I have works." Show
me your faith without your[a] works, and I will show you my faith
by my[b] works... 19 You believe that there is one God. You do
well. Even the demons believe—and tremble! 20 But do you want
to know, O foolish man, that faith without works is dead?[c]21 Was
not Abraham our father justified by works when he offered Isaac
his son on the altar?22 Do you see that faith was working together
with his works, and by works faith was made perfect? 23 And the
Scripture was fulfilled which says, "Abraham believed God, and it
was accounted to him for righteousness."[d] And he was called the
friend of God.24 You see then that a man is justified by works, and
not by faith only.
25 Likewise, was not Rahab the harlot also justified by works when
she received the messengers and sent *them* out another way?
26 For as the body without the spirit is dead, so faith without works
is dead also.

1. **Hebrews 11:1 NLT**
"Faith is the confidence that what we hope for will actually happen; it gives us assurance about things we cannot see."
2. **Ephesians 2:8 AMP**
"For it is by grace [God's remarkable compassion and favor drawing you to Christ] that you have been saved [actually delivered from judgment and given eternal life] *through faith*. And this [salvation] is not of yourselves [not through your own effort], but it is the [undeserved, gracious] gift of God."
Joshua 10:13-14
On the day the LORD gave the Israelites victory over the Amorites, Joshua prayed to the LORD in front of all the people of Israel. He said, "Let the sun stand still over Gibeon, and the moon over the valley of Aijalon."
So the sun stood still, and the moon stopped, till the nation avenged itself on its enemies, as it is written in the Book of Jashar. The sun stopped in the middle of the sky and delayed going down about a full day. There has never been a day like it before or since, a day when the LORD listened to a human being. Surely the LORD was fighting for Israel!

Chapter 7

Living in peace

> **Romans 12: 16- 18** 16 Live in harmony with one another. Do not be proud, but be willing to associate with people of low position. Do not be conceited. 17 Do not repay anyone evil for evil. Be careful to do what is right in the eyes of everyone. 18 If it is possible, as far as it depends on you, live at peace with everyone.

Living in peace is a learning process! As Christian people, we must learn to live in peace despite the circumstances or dynamics of what we are facing. There is calamity, despair, heartbreak, and pain all around us. Fret not for evil things that you see or experience because No weapon formed against me shall prosper. There is a great need to trust and depend completely on God because he deeply cares for us. The scripture teaches us to cast our cares upon Christ because he cares for us. The scripture also teaches us that the cares of this world will snuff out the very love of God. Therefore, the process begins with our trust and faith in God.

Christians if you want to be successful, you have to work hard at listening and respond correctly to the word and the spirit of God. The major reason we have not been successful in football, basketball, school or just life. We as Christians often live in despair because we are always a second or two behind in making plays or decisions, meaning that we are not available to hear the voice of God.

There is a process of living and learning God's voice. The scripture teaches us that warning come before destruction. How can the warnings from God happen if you don't have a good relationship with him? We have to be ready at all times so that nothing evil comes upon us unaware. This is a part of the process of living in peace. When we have brokenness in our lives there is no hope for peace. There is no peace without a relationship with God. If we want peace, we must Fellowship with God, in our fellowship with God we have the opportunity to live in total tranquility. Fellowship with God is essential to peaceful natural and spiritual living.

Are you ready to Receive?

In order to receive everything that God has for you, you must be in the mind of receiving. In order to be in the mind of receiving, it's going to require a lot of work. Our minds carry so much toxic waste that we must empty immediately. The beginning of emptying out starts with:

2 Corinthians 10:5 Casting down imaginations, and every high thing that exalteth itself against the knowledge of God, and bringing into captivity every thought to the obedience of Christ. Philippians 2:5-11 is a strong reminder of where our mind should revolve around.

Philippians 2:5-11
5 Let this mind be in you, which was also in Christ Jesus:
6 Who, being in the form of God, thought it not robbery to be equal with God:
7 But made himself of no reputation, and took upon him the form of a servant, and was made in the likeness of men:
8 And being found in fashion as a man, he humbled himself, and became obedient unto death, even the death of the cross.
9 Wherefore God also hath highly exalted him, and given him a name which is above every name:
10 That at the name of Jesus every knee should bow, of things in heaven, and things in earth, and things under the earth;
11 And that every tongue should confess that Jesus Christ is Lord, to the glory of God the Father.
Hebrews 10:35 So do not throw away this confidence trust in the Lord. Remember the great reward it brings you!

Chapter 8

The Champion inside of you

> **Deuteronomy 20:4**
> For the LORD your God is he who goes with you to fight for you against your enemies, to give you the victory.

The champion in you has far greater influence than you can ever imagine. There is an inner being called a spirit that lives inside of you, so powerful that it can conquer all of your fears, all of your disappointments, and cause you to be triumphed over anything that stands in your way. Think about it like this before you were ever conceived inside of your mother's womb, God said I knew you. I don't know about you, but that's powerful!

Jeremiah 1:5

"Before I formed you in the womb I knew you, before you were born I set you apart; I appointed you as a prophet to the nations."
This very scripture validates that God knew who we were long before we did and just because you don't know who you are, or who you were created to be, God knows cares about our present and our future.

Why did God make the earth and us along with it? He doesn't really need us, so why did he create anything?

Great question and you're not the first to ask this. King David asked essentially the same thing:

"When I consider your heavens, the work of your fingers ... what is man that you are mindful of him, the son of man that you care for him?" (Psalm 8:3-4).

Why did God make us? To answer that, we need to know three things:

1. It wasn't because he needed us: "The God who made the world and everything in it is not served by human hands, *as if he needed anything*" (Acts 17:24-25).

And he didn't make us because he was lonely. Long before we were here, God already had "company" with his Son and the Holy Spirit, as referred to in Genesis 1:26, "Let us make man in *our* own image." Think of that for just a few moments. God created us in his own image. You were created in the very image of God, if that doesn't make you feel like a champion I'm not sure if anything will. To know that I was created in the image of the Almighty God speaks volume to whom I am, and who I am destined to become. And He didn't make us because he needed his ego fed. It's not like God made us to satisfy some craving to be worshiped. God is totally secured in who He is without us.

2. Despite not needing us, God chose to create us anyway out of his great love: A love that every born again believer should strive to obtain. Often times, we allow petty insignificant things to prevent us from loving one another and it last for weeks, months, and even years. In fact, we often forget all reasoning behind why we fall out of love with one another and forgiveness is often lost forever.

"I have loved you with an everlasting love" (Jeremiah 31:3). Yes, God loved us *before he even created us*. It's impossible to get our heads around that idea, but it's true; that's what "everlasting" love means.

God *is* love (1 John 4:8), and because of that love and his wonderful creativity, he made us so we can enjoy all that he is and all that he's done.

3. God created us to fulfill his eternal plan. I could write pages and pages about this, but God, in his infinite wisdom, chose to make us a part of his eternal plan. What part do we play in this plan? Well, the Bible is full of instructions for how we should live our lives. But here are a few key verses to remember:

4. **"Love the Lord your God with all your heart and with all your soul and with all your strength" (Deuteronomy 6:5).**

5. **"Love your neighbor as yourself" (Matthew 22:39).**

6. **"We are God's workmanship, created in Christ Jesus to do good works, which God prepared in advance for us to do" (Ephesians 2:10).**

We're also part of the war between God and Satan, and God's ultimate plan to defeat Satan. By putting our faith in God, we can defeat Satan and his lies (see Ephesians 6:10-18).

Finally, perhaps the most important part we play in God's eternal plan is to point people to eternal life with God through his Son, Jesus Christ. The Bible calls this our "ministry of reconciliation" (2 Corinthians 5:18-19). That's why we're here. But it's also important to note that we have a *choice* in all of this. When God created us, he didn't make us pawns in some cosmic chess game. We're not his toy soldiers. God gives us freedom of choice. Bottom line: God may not need us, but we certainly need him. I hope you've made the choice to put your trust completely in Him and play an exciting part in his loving, eternal plan for your life. In making this choice, you have aligned yourself with a force that no man or demon in hell can come against.

Isaiah 54:17

No weapon forged against you will prevail, and you will refute every tongue that accuses you. This is the heritage of the servants of the LORD, and this is their vindication from me," declares the LORD.

I take confidence in knowing that because of this scripture I need not to vindicate myself. My vindication comes from God as he has declared it to be so in his word. If you are a new believer, it's important to know that all types of forces of evil are going to come up against you but God gives us vindication through them all. Be of good courage that no matter what it looks like, we must hold fast to his word and gain strength in knowing that God knows all and He cares for us despite who hurts or misuses us. God will provide the vindication, all I have to do is put it in his hands and trust in him, and he will definitely do the rest.

Philippians 4:13Amplified Bible (AMP)

[13] **I can do all things [which He has called me to do] through Him who strengthens *and* empowers me [to fulfill His purpose—I am self-sufficient in Christ's sufficiency; I am ready for anything and equal to anything through Him who infuses me with inner strength and confident peace.]**

Remember to always hold fast and take confidence in knowing that God has given us the power to overcome the enemy.

John Steward breaks it down like this, though the Bible presents the Devil as a powerful and cunning opponent, it also tells us that Christians can have victory over this enemy.

You are from God, little children, and have overcome them; because greater is He who is in you than he who is in the world (1 John 4:4).

We know that those who are born of God do not sin, but the one who was born of God protects them, and the evil one does not touch them (1 John 5:18).

Our Own Choice

It must be emphasized that Satan cannot make the believer do anything! When a Christian sins, it is because they have chosen to sin. It is not the responsibility of anyone else. Satan can entice someone to sin, but he cannot force them to sin. It all depends on our will power.

In Christ

Satan cannot recapture that person who is "in Christ." Therefore, Satan is a defeated enemy, one who ultimately will be thrown into the lake of fire. However, until that time, he is still very active in our world. Consequently, the believer must take the proper steps to win victory over this enemy.

Some Victories, Some Defeats

While believers are living in this world-system, and battling the attacks of the Devil, it is possible to achieve temporary victories over this foe. These victories can only come through faith in Christ. Though victory is always possible, occasional defeat will occur, if the believer fails to do their part. Though these defeats do not affect the final outcome, they can hinder a person's Christian testimony, as well as their spiritual growth. Therefore, we need to discover how victory over the Devil can be achieved.

Steps To Take

The following are some steps that the believer should take.

1. Understand Our Enemy

It is important that we understand who our enemy is. We need to know what he is able to do, his limitations, and the various ways in which he works. The Bible says.

Put on the full armor of God so that you can take your stand against the Devil's schemes (Ephesians 6:11)

This can only be found from a study of God's Word. Satan takes advantage of those who are spiritually immature and ignorant in God's righteousness.

2. Know His Methods

We also need to know how the Devil works - we are not to be ignorant of his methods. The Bible says.

that no advantage may be gained over us by Satan: for we are not ignorant of his devices (2 Corinthians 2:11).

3. Test The Spirits

Believers have a responsibility to test the spirits, and know if its God. Evil spirits will give off evil. When in doubt follow the Holy Scriptures and see what it reveals.

Beloved, do not believe every spirit, but test the spirits to see whether they are from God; for many false prophets have gone out into the world (1 John 4:1).

This is something we must actively do; we are not to sit by passively.

4. Be Actively Watching

The Bible tells us to be watching for these tricks of the Devil.

Be sober, be watchful: your adversary the Devil, as a roaring lion, walks about, seeking whom he may devour (1 Peter 5:8).

We should be on guard against his attacks.

5. Resist Him When He Comes

The Bible tells believers to resist the Devil.

Be subject therefore unto God; but resist the Devil, and he will flee from you (James 4:7).

"Resist" has the idea of withstand, or to stand our ground. By standing our ground, Satan can be overcome. John wrote to believers.

I am writing to you, fathers, because you know Him who is from the beginning. I am writing to you, young people, because you have conquered the evil one (1 John 2:13).

6. Realize Weak Areas

Every human being has areas in their life in which they are much vulnerable. Satan knows these areas. Consequently, believers should be alert from attacks in the areas where they are the weakest. The Bible commands us not to give any opportunity to the Devil to work.

neither give place to the Devil (Ephesians 4:27).

7. Not In Our Strength

We learn a valuable lesson from Michael, the archangel in dealing with Satan.

But when the archangel Michael, contending with the Devil, disputed about the body of Moses, he did not presume to pronounce a reviling judgment upon him, but said, "The Lord rebuke you" (Jude 9).

We should not personally defy the devil. We need to respect his power and should neither underestimate nor overestimate him.

8. Avoid The Situation

As much as possible, believers should avoid any situation that can cause them to sin - they should separate themselves from the source of the temptation of the devil.

abstain from every form of evil (1 Thessalonians 5:22).

By separating themselves from a particular sin, both morally and geographically, a temporary victory can be won. However, all victories are only temporary because temptation will always come as long as we are in these mortal bodies.

9. Put On The Full Armor Of God

The believer has authority over the unseen realm by putting on the spiritual armor that God has provided.

For our struggle is not against enemies of blood and flesh, but against the rulers, against the authorities, against the cosmic powers of this present darkness, against the spiritual forces of evil in the heavenly places. Therefore take up the whole armor of God, so that you may be able to withstand on that evil day, and having done everything, to stand firm (Ephesians 6:12,13).

The armor consists of spiritual realities that believers need to appropriate every day. By daily surrendering ourselves to the Lord, and placing our faith in Him, we can take advantage of these spiritual realities because it is a spiritual battle in which we are fighting. The Bible says.

The weapons we fight with are not the weapons of the world. On the contrary, they have divine power to demolish strongholds (2 Corinthians 10:4).

These realities are compared to the outfit a Roman soldier would wear.

The Belt Of Truth

One of our weapons of warfare in the spiritual realm is the belt of truth.

Stand therefore, and fasten the belt of truth around your waist (Ephesians 6:14).

The belt of truth refers to the truth of the Word of God as well as the truthfulness we should display in our daily lives. Since Satan is always a liar (John 8:44) we need to concern ourselves with the truth.

The Coat Of Righteousness

We are told to put on the breastplate, or coat, of righteousness.

and put on the breastplate of righteousness (Ephesians 6:14).

This refers to doing the right thing. We can only do the right thing after we have put on the righteousness of Jesus Christ. This happens when a person trusts solely on Christ as Savior.

Therefore, since we are justified by faith, we have peace with God through our Lord Jesus Christ (Romans 5:1).

Believers are now able to do that which is right in the sight of the Lord.

The Sandals Of Preparation

Our feet also need to be covered by God's armor.

As shoes for your feet put on whatever will make you ready to proclaim the gospel of peace (Ephesians 6:15).

This speaks of spreading the good news about Jesus. Our job is to testify to the lost that there is forgiveness of sin in the person of Jesus Christ. We are to be ready to go wherever He will send us. Those who do this are said to have "beautiful feet."

And how are they to proclaim Him unless they are sent? As it is written, "How beautiful are the feet of those who bring good news!" (Romans 10:15).

The Shield Of Faith

When the wicked one attacks, there is a shield for believers.

With all of these, take the shield of faith, with which you will be able to quench all the flaming arrows of the evil one (Ephesians 6:16).

We are to place our faith in God's promises when we are attacked with fear and doubt.

The Helmet Of Salvation

The Bible also speaks of armor that protects the head.

Take the helmet of salvation (Ephesians 6:17).

The head speaks of knowledge. We need to understand that we have been given assurance of salvation seeing that it is God who will carry us through. While Satan wants to keep believers ignorant of these truths, and to keep them in continual doubt, Jesus wants to set them free.

So if the Son makes you free, you will be free indeed (John 8:36).

The Sword Of The Spirit

The scripture now speaks of an offensive weapon in the believers armor.

the sword of the Spirit, which is the word of God (Ephesians 6:17).

The believer needs to understand how to use the Bible effectively when the attacks of the enemy comes.

9. Maintain Constant Communication With God

We are also told to constantly be in prayer to God.

Pray in the Spirit at all times in every prayer and supplication. To that end keep alert and always persevere in supplication for all the saints (Ephesians 6:18).

Talking to God on a constant basis can help stop the progress of the devil. Elsewhere we are commanded to pray unceasingly.

pray continually (1 Thessalonians 5:17).

10. Realize Whose Family You Are Part Of

The Bible speaks of two families of humanity - those who are the children of God, and those who are the children of the devil. Those who are in the family of God have their lives molded after Him. Those who belong to the devil act like their spiritual father. Believers ought to realize which family they belong to and act accordingly. The Bible says.

for everyone born of God overcomes the world. This is the victory that has overcome the world, even our faith (1 John 5:4).

11. Rest In God's Promises

Finally, we need to rest in the promises of God. Satan has been overcome and the victory is ours!

No testing has overtaken you that is not common to everyone. God is faithful, and He will not let you be tested beyond your strength, but with the testing He will also provide the way out so that you may be able to endure it (1 Corinthians 10:13).

Paul said.

I can do all things through Him who strengthens me (Philippians 4:13).

Summary

The Bible gives us a way in which we can deal with the Devil. Though, the Devil has been defeated, and eventually will be thrown into the lake of fire, he is still actively spreading evil. Christians need to understand who he is, and what he is able to do while he is still active. As long as one looks to Christ, victory can be achieved.

In addition to this awesome information, there is still yet one more important ingredient one must possess. This ingredient is Obedience to God, his Holy Word. Obedience is the key to the success of any Christian. Obeying God's word opens the door of a believer.

Chapter 9

The Enemy in you

> **Proverbs 24:16**
> For the righteous falls seven times and rises again, but the wicked stumble in times of calamity.

The enemy in you is very powerful and often goes undetected or recognized by the individual for a number of reasons. I believe the number one reason is because as Christians, we believe that we should not face any obstacles, hardships, trials, or tribulations in life. I believe because of this mindset and belief as Christians we are exposed to suffering. The suffering is unbearable because we have a sense of entitlement as Christians, as Christians we expect God to shield us from all adversity. Therefore, when adversity does come into our lives we find ourselves devastated, and overwhelmed by the calamity shock and destruction of it. However, the enemies inside of us known as our flesh is very powerful even more powerful than Satan himself. Imagine if your flesh and Satan teams up against your soul, your destination is straight to hell.

Romans 7:17-18

17 In that case, it is no longer I who do it, but it is sin living in me that does it. 18 I know that nothing goodlives in me, that is, in my flesh; for I have the desire to do what is good, but I cannot carry it out. 19For I do not do the good I want to do. Instead, I keep on doing the evil I do not want to do....

I believe that we somehow forget that we have an enemy to our souls running wild on the earth loose. The fact of the matter is no one wants to accept that there is an enemy lurking inside of them, but certainly there is. It's commonly known as our flesh; it controls and dictates to us how our life should be and when things don't go according to how the flesh desires it to go, then all Hell breaks loose inside of us. As fleshly people, we want whatever our eye gages say we deserve, no matter who we have to steal from, cheat, or kill to have it. It's what we want and we will do whatever it takes to get it. It could be in the form of a career, a home, a car, a man, woman, or whatever it is we feel like we deserve. Our selfish desires are so powerful inside of us like a crazy burst of energy until we get it, and now just like a little kid we are off to some other adventure that we see, think and feel like we deserve to have. We are our own worst enemy simply because we allow our flesh to control and dictate our actions. Below is how the Holy Scriptures categorizes it.

Romans 12:2-3 Do not be conformed to this world, but be transformed by the renewing of your mind. Then you will be able to discern what is the good, pleasing, and perfect will of God. 3For by the grace given me I say to every one of you: Do not think of yourself more highly than you ought, but think of yourself with sober judgment, according to the measure of faith God has given you.

STOP, LISTEN & BREATH:

This section is designed for salient points and take a ways from what you just read!

Notes

_____

_____

_____

_____

_____

_____

_____

_____

_____

_____

_____

_____

_____

    There is a supernatural war that goes on inside of us that we must learn how to defeat with the power that we have been given from God. The enemy that lives inside of us has the power to cause mass destruction in our lives. For instance, we build cravings inside of ourselves such as a craving to smoke cigarettes, marijuana, alcohol indulgences, sex whether it fornication or adultery or simple things like overeating or using profanity. These things dictates and even control our minds and ultimately our lives.

    When people who love us sees us traveling down the wrong road trying to stir us or guide us in the right direction we become indignant, pious, rebellious and often refuse to listen or be anywhere around them. These are often the very people who are praying for our victory over these harmful addictions or destructive ways of living. However, the enemy within us is so strong within us to the point that it blinds or impairs our way of thinking.

2 Corinthians 10:3-4

3 For though we live in the flesh, we do not wage war according to the flesh. 4 The weapons of our warfare are not the weapons of the world. Instead, they have divine power to demolish strongholds. 5We tear down arguments, and every presumption set up against the knowledge of God; and we take captive every thought to make it obedient to Christ....

STOP, LISTEN & BREATH:

This section is designed for salient points and take a ways from what you just read!

Notes:

_____

_____

_____

_____

_____

_____

_____

_____

Chapter 10

Salvation 101

Romans 10:9-10 New International Version (NIV)
9 If you declare with your mouth, "Jesus is Lord," and believe in your heart that God raised him from the dead, you will be saved. 10 For it is with your heart that you believe and are justified, and it is with your mouth that you profess your faith and are saved.

Salvation is sometimes viewed as a very complicated and complex decision for people to make. I believe it goes back to the lack of knowledge. When we don't truly understand what is being asked or required of us it becomes difficult to make a good wholesome decision, especially one as important as this one.

My experience in having this conversation with people who aren't saved, they truly don't understand what salvation is. My most common response to this is that people often feel that they have to make some drastic changes in their life and that isn't all together true. There are some necessary changes that you have to make like open your heart and mind up to receive God's Love, his grace and mercies as well gaining insight on his principles that we all must follow.

Christians sometimes lack the ability to live a life that is without spot or wrinkles. This causes a strain on the non-believer's decision about being saved. They are looking at people who are imperfect and looking for perfection. I believe this is one of the greatest obstacles. I view this as being an obstacle because we as Christians don't do a good job in letting others know that we are not perfect people. The only reason a lot of Christians are viewed as being perfect is based on God's ability to hide us in him. When we are hidden in God, we are able to be viewed as perfect in the eyesight of man. God says that if any man says he is without sin, he is a liar and truth isn't found in him. God also says that we are like filthy rags in the eye sight of God. The Holy Scriptures also lets us know that we are clay and that God is the potter, so we must stay on the potters will until we are perfected by God. This means that once you receive salvation there is yet so much work that needs to be done.

Paul's life was a wonderful example of the work needed to make the changes to become Christ like. Paul once known as Saul was the chief persecutor of the children of God. Saul as he was known was relentless when it came to persecuting the children of God. I mean Saul made life for the Christians pure torture. Christian feared the name of Saul. Saul was responsible for the death of Steven who was doing the work of building the kingdom of God. One day, while on his was to Damascus to persecute and perhaps even kill more Christians, Paul had an encounter with Jesus. This encounter changed his entire way of thinking much like what happens with us once we meet Jesus and know where our greatest source of power lies. This encounter with Jesus was so miraculous, that his name was changed and he is credited for writing the majority of the New Testament. Wow, what an amazing story, but so is your story. The Holy Scriptures says, eyes have not seen nor have ears heard, nor has it entered in the mind of man the things that God has in stored for us, his people.

Jeremiah 29:11-12

11For I know the plans that I have for you,' declares the LORD, 'plans for welfare and not for calamity to give you a future and a hope. 12'Then you will call upon Me and come and pray to Me, and I will listen to you....

Salvation is the key that unlocks the door to your God given call. This will never take place if you refuse to open up your heart and mind and believe that Christ Jesus death, burial and resurrection is true. Brothers and sisters, if you believe these simple truths then you are saved. Let know man tell you otherwise. There is a myth out there that says once saved always saved. I don't agree with that and here is why.

I believe that we have to fight daily to remain saved similar to that of a strict diet. If you want to lose weight, then you have to work on it daily, if you decide I'm sick and tired of watching what I eat, then you're going to eat everything in sight. This attitude will affect your weight lost plan.

No matter how much you want to lose weight, if you're not working on it you're not going to lose weight. I think that's a common practice or common knowledge. Then how can one say that once saved always saved. Another simple analogy would be that, if continue to do all the things that I know aren't pleasing in my natural mother and fathers sight, do they continue to do that which is good for me or do they eventually say enough is enough, and they no longer extend the loving and kind hands unto me. This type of thinking may not be the same for everyone but God's word says, I will turn him over to himself.

Often time, you will see our humanistic view of ourselves as being good to the degree we think more highly of ourselves than we should. The Holy Scriptures warns against people thinking more highly of themselves than they should. Thinking more highly of yourself than you should put us in a place where we lose out all the way around with both man and God. For me I don't want to run the risk of believing once saved always saved because it puts me in a place of getting too relaxed and comfortable.

I don't think there's anything wrong to be relaxed about something but never get too comfortable with your salvation to the point that you feel like you cannot lose it. This takes me in to my next point of reference relationship with God and man.

What is salvation? What is the Christian doctrine of salvation?"

Answer: Salvation is deliverance from danger or suffering. To save is to deliver or protect. The word carries the idea of victory, health, or preservation. Sometimes, the Bible uses the words *saved* or *salvation* to refer to temporal, physical deliverance, such as Paul's deliverance from prison (Philippians 1:19).

More often, the word "salvation" concerns an eternal, spiritual deliverance. When Paul told the Philippian jailer what he must do to be saved, he was referring to the jailer's eternal destiny (Acts 16:30-31). Jesus equated being saved with entering the kingdom of God (Matthew 19:24-25).

What are we saved *from*? In the Christian doctrine of salvation, we are saved from "wrath," that is, from God's judgment of sin (Romans 5:9; 1 Thessalonians 5:9). Our sin has separated us from God, and the consequence of sin is death (Romans 6:23). Biblical salvation refers to our deliverance from the consequence of sin and therefore involves the removal of sin.

Who does the saving? Only God can remove sin and deliver us from sin's penalty (2 Timothy 1:9; Titus3:5).

How does God save? In the Christian doctrine of salvation, God has rescued us through Christ (John 3:17). Specifically, it was Jesus' death on the cross and subsequent resurrection that achieved our salvation (Romans 5:10; Ephesians 1:7). Scripture is clear that salvation is the gracious, undeserved gift of God (Ephesians 2:5, 8) and is only available through faith in Jesus Christ(Acts4:12).

How do we receive salvation? We are saved by *faith*. First, we must *hear* the gospel—the good news of Jesus' death and resurrection (Ephesians 1:13). Then, we must *believe*—fully trust the Lord Jesus (Romans 1:16). This involves repentance, a changing of mind about sin and Christ (Acts3:19), and calling on the name of the Lord

(Romans10:9-10, 13)

A definition of the Christian doctrine of salvation would be "The deliverance, by the grace of God, from eternal punishment for sin which is granted to those who accept by faith God's conditions of repentance and faith in the Lord Jesus." Salvation is available in Jesus alone (John 14:6; Acts 4:12) and is dependent on God alone for provision, assurance, and security.

STOP, LISTEN & BREATH:

This section is designed for salient points and take a ways from what you just read!

Notes:

_____

_____

_____

_____

_____

_____

_____

_____

_____

_____

_____

_____

_____

Chapter 11

Relationships

> **Proverb 13:20** Walk with the wise and become wise, for a companion of fools suffers harm.

Relationships are very critical when you decide to turn your life over to God. Often time we see this to be true with criminals who get out of jail. The recommendation is to not go back in to the same environment or relationships you had prior to going to jail. These relationships are often a threat to the individual going back to jail. The recidivism rate for juveniles and adults returning back to prison are extremely for this exact reason. Taking a common sense approach to this also gives clarity. Everyone knows that people have influence; this is especially true with negative influences. How often have you heard the statement birds of a feather flock together? More often than not this is true. So, people who love you will say please don't hang out with this one or that one because they are going to have a negative influence on your decisions both minor and major.

Building strong positive relationships are critical to your Christian walk and salvation for this exact reason because the power of influence is always working. The definition of insanity is if you always do what you have always done then you're going to always get the same results. This is true when we decide to follow Jesus with our whole heart. There are going to be some people who won't believe or accept you or support the decisions you have made because they don't want to see you successful. A true friend is one that loves you like a brother. This friend will lead, guide and direct your life to follow after Christ Jesus. A true friend will support you doing anything positive unless they have a hidden agenda or motive.

These are just a few reasons that friendships are critical to your journey. Friends will either build you up or tear you down. In the opening of this book, there was a poem, I love to read. The builder's poem speaks about how strategic and skillful you must be to build a house. This is true with relationships because you have to be skillfully trained to build and maintain healthy and wholesome relationships, if not you will be sleeping with the enemy and never know it. I use this statement because most people won't be caught sleeping with the enemy. There we must be mindful and watchful over our Christian journey. This is equally important with connecting with people of like mind as you or even higher. Connecting with people that have the strength, the courage, and the ability to strategically fight off the enemy of your soul. The bible talks about how evil communications corrupts good manner. This is another reason to choose very carefully of whom to let into your inner circle.

The Holy Scriptures also talks about man not being an island to him or herself. So we cannot simple say that we can make it without other people. Relationships are so critical to your growth. Relationships cause us to grow and become closer to God. If we are not cable of growing relationships with people here on earth how then can we make a relationship with God. Relationships require work, understanding and lots of time and energy. This same process is as equally important with God. How do we begin a relationship with God? First, by getting to know who he is to me and my life. Allowing, his Holy Spirit to freely enter me with the evidence of speaking in tongues. Without God's Holy Spirit it's impossible to have a quality relationship with God or man.

STOP, LISTEN & BREATH:

This section is designed for salient points and take a ways from what you just read!

Notes

_____

_____

_____

_____

_____

_____

_____

_____

_____

_____

_____

Chapter 12

Fear

> **Psalm 56:11** In God I trust; I shall not be afraid. What can man do to me?

Fear is one of the greatest defenses that Satan uses against the child of God. I know the reason he uses it! He uses it because if he can get the child of God's faith to be weakened through fear of the unknown or fear of what we sees, he has won a small victory. This small yet insignificant victory can cause a life time of loses in the win lost Colum. In this journey called life, we will face obstacles, circumstances situations, and dangers that are breath taking and even at times it may appear hopeless. I'm instantly reminded of Job. Job faced adversity based on his character, integrity and relationship with God.

The story of Job is one of great adversity and great hope for one's trust in the Lord. The story is a bit puzzling and I recommend that every believer reads this story. The story is one that I admire because in the eyes of God he saw Job as his champion. The story speaks about how Satan was in heaven one day hanging out and the Lord challenged him. Understanding Satan's every move and thoughts, God proved to Satan of his power. Although, Satan should know the vastness of God's power, one would have to question why he took on a challenge like this. The challenge was, have you considered my servant Job? God being fully aware that Satan's mission is to destroy anything and anyone who loves God. God knows that Satan goes to and fro on the earth seeking whom he may devour. Knowing this was Satan's mission, and I believe God wanted him to finally recognize that he was no match for God. However, being Satan and with all of his pride and vanity, he jumped to the challenge. We know Satan to be very wise and cunning but what

I don't understand is why he would take on this challenge knowing that this could not and would not end in his favor. One would think that he had enough from the fall from heaven. The curious thing is that Satan isn't revealed by name or situation that is often portrayed in the bible like this. However, if I were Satan I would have gracefully bowed out of this challenge. So in dealing with the topic fear here, it is worthy to note that we have God, Satan and Job. God issues a challenge to prove to Satan Job's loyalty. Satan believes that he can convince Job to doubt God if he attacks his family, his finances and his flesh. This is an amazing story of a great man of God losing everything but yet trusting in God. The fear of losing your family, worldly possession and even your health can potential break the greatest of men here in this story as we see Job bent but not broken. Job's current wife even recommends that he curse God and die. Job rebukes his wife, calls her foolish and continues to trust in the Almighty God his ultimate vindicator. No matter what the enemy put before Job he serviced and continued to serve God with his whole heart. This is a true testament of his faith in God if we all could only have Job like faith where we remain fearless and unmoved by the tricks of the enemy.

This topic of fear goes much deeper than what really meets the eye. Often times, it's hard for people to admit that they are afraid of something. Pride won't allow you to open up and say I'm afraid of what might happen or I'm just plan afraid.

2 Timothy 1:7 For God has not given us a spirit of fear and timidity, but of power, love, and self-discipline.

I love this scripture in particular because I find myself quoting it a lot. I guess you can call me a scary cat because this scripture stays on repeat for me. I find great comfort in quoting this scripture anytime I find myself in trouble or doubting myself for some reason or another. Sometimes, I quote this scripture once and sometimes I find myself quoting this scripture twenty times or more depending on what I'm dealing with. The scripture is very powerful and it works well. I find myself quoting it multiple times because my mind is constantly giving me fearful thoughts, so as you can see it's not that scripture doesn't work the first time it's just that I have to continue to battle the thoughts that comes up in my mind. The funny thing is I have understood the power of God's word for over 30 years but right now, this scripture is on speed dial. My kids know and use this scripture a lot as well. I taught them this scripture because of the power that dwells in it.

One really good example of me and my children using this scripture is when we travel by air. My kids know that before they step their foot on an airplane they are supposed to touch the outside of the airplane with their hands and whisper a silent pray for traveling safety through God's grace and mercy. Then, once you sit down a prayer of thanks giving should take place, a rededication of their soul is given to God and full and total control of their life is given back to God. Normally, this is my prayer before we take off. Oftentimes, they have no clue that I'm saying this pray, because I wasn't sure if they knew the magnitude of being 30,000 plus feet in the air without any control. So, this was often my prayer simply because I wasn't going to put our lives in anyone's hands other than Gods hands. My confidence belongs to a powerful God who created the heavens and the earth. While in the air, sometimes we experience turbulence and oh boy, the scripture was definitely over worked to ease my fears. I find myself in complete control after quoting this scripture; the scripture simply wipes away my fears and gives me reaffirmed confidence in the God that I serve.

STOP, LISTEN & BREATH:

This section is designed for salient points and take a ways from what you just read!

Notes:

_____

_____

_____

Chapter 13

Death

> **John 14 :1-3** "Let not your heart be troubled; you believe in God, believe also in Me. 2 In My Father's house are many mansions; if it were not so, I would have told you. I go to prepare a place for you. 3 And if I go and prepare a place for you, I will…

The death of a love one or close friend has a tendency to cut deep into your core belief, and it's at this time we question Gods plans and even if he is moving on our behalf or not. During death our faith has to be increased ten times greater to understand why Gods determined end for that love has come and if it's even justified. There is no really good rhyme or reason that we can tell ourselves or others as to why the decision was made and that persons determined end had come.

We often say to be absent from the body is to be present with the Lord, or God knew what was best. These are all true, but often hard and even difficult to absorb when dealing with the death of a love one, but nothing shall separate us from the love of God not death, nor life.

Romans 8:35-39

³⁵ **Can anything separate us from the love Christ has for us? Can troubles or problems or sufferings? If we have no food or clothes, if we are in danger, or even if death comes—can any of these things separate us from Christ's love? ³⁶ As it is written in the Scriptures:**

³⁷ **But in all these things we have full victory through God who showed his love for us. ³⁸⁻³⁹ Yes, I am sure that nothing can separate us from the love God has for us. Not death, not life, not angels, not ruling spirits, nothing now, nothing in the future, no powers,**

nothing above us, nothing below us, or anything else in the whole world will ever be able to separate us from the love of God that is in Christ Jesus our Lord.

Psalm 44:22
"For you we are in danger of death all the time. People think we are worth no more than sheep to be killed."

Dealing with death is a complicated set of circumstance that can really weigh on a person. I don't care if you're saved, sanctified and filled with the Holy Spirit it's grueling for anyone. We are all human beings who are often led, guided and sometimes driven by our emotions. Death can be very complicated because it's the unknown and that individual loved one whom we have had the pleasure of knowing is no longer with us. There are so many unanswered questions we want to know about the person who is no longer with us. These questions often extended from did they make heaven, did they suffer, how do we make it without them, or where do we go from here? Questions that don't often have answers that we understand and even want to hear especially if you don't have a basic understanding of who God is and what the Holy scriptures reveals.

I often think of my loved ones who have gone on to the next life. The one that weighs the heaviest on me is my grandmother, Mrs. Johnnie Mae aka Nanny. Oh, how I long to sit and chat with her about life and a number of other things. As long as I could remember she has been a very solid part of my life, it's like one day I woke up and she was there and never left. She would always make me feel so loved and safe as she did to all of her children and grandchildren. I would like to think that we had a special bond like no one else did.

I remember how when I went off to college she would often send me these huge boxes of food and things that I missed from home but couldn't get from where I was. She would always ball up money and place it in my hand and say Nanny loves you. My eyes are tearing up as I type these words and it's been over ten years my grandmother passed away. Well, that shows that it's ok to reminisce and reflect back on loved ones who have gone on to be with the Lord.

I strongly believe that their memories will forever be cherished in your eyes, but we have to move on past the hurt or pain caused by the individual or the pain of their absence. The Holy Scriptures talks about to be absent from the body is to be present with the Lord. This does provide some level of comfort to a person that understands God's purpose and plan in their life. To the person that does not understand, it's going to be an even tougher road ahead for them.

One bit of advice I would like to add for the born again believer about death is that this is what we worship for, to one day be with the Lord. When a loved one passes away and we are confident of the life that they have lived then it's a time of rejoicing. In fact, what's the point of going to church all of your life or even some of your life, and still you are afraid to death. The whole point is to get to heaven. I know that none of us is ready to go today but why go to church and live a righteous and holy life if you are too afraid to die or why it's too hard to live with your loved ones death.

Time heals all wounds, we just have to remain faithful and be encouraged with what God has promised he will bring to pass. Jesus said that I go to prepare a place for you, so that where I am you will be also. He said if it were not so I would have told you.

John 14 1:4 "Do not let your hearts be troubled. You believe in God; believe also in me. 2My Father's house has many rooms; if that were not so, would I have told you that I am going there to prepare a place for you? 3And if I go and prepare a place for you, I will come back and take you to be with me that you also may be where I am. 4You know the way to the place where I am going."

On my Christian journey I learned the importance of being a builder. I choose to be a builder based on the intent behind the poem Builders shown in the first start of the book. Poems like that one keeps me rooted and grounded on the bigger picture in life. The poem helps me focus on the things that are important like building people up rather than tearing them down. Christian people can keep up sometimes that we forget God's mission and focus totally on our own mission. God has given each of us a special mission here on earth that we are assigned to do. This mission is not complete on until we face death.

On my journey, I see all types of Christian people like most of the readers have. I'm confident that you can make reference to this poem as well. I am of the opinion that some Christian folk spend entirely too much time trying to get the beam out of your eye when they have a smote in their own eyes. In other words, we often focus so much attention on what a person is doing wrong rather than praying and supporting them to live a productive Christian life. The scriptures talks about seeing your brother or sister keeper in err and praying for them. Have you ever found yourself doing more criticizing than building up?

I find it easy to sit around and secretly criticize others without them ever really knowing just how you feel. What benefit is that other than to get a free laugh from another person's weakness or down fall. I see this happening a lot. I work hard at not being a part of such gossip. In fact, I have been criticized for leaving services as soon as it ends and arriving just in time for it to start. However, no one has ever asked me about my rational behind my behavior, yet they would rather secretly assume that I don't care about people, or I don't want to be available for the Lord's use. All of this is nowhere near the truth.

The real truth is that I discovered that it's better to distance myself from some Christian people even leaders that my mind may steer clear from additional unclean, impure, unholy thoughts piled by others belief or assumptions. I discovered that there are those that are in leadership who love to gossip and have chatter about others who are no longer there to speak on their own behalf. I feel confident in writing this because there are chances that the people I have observed doing this don't really support me and on top of that they won't read this body of work based on their opinion of who they perceive the writer to be. I know that God has so much in store for his chosen people.

Proverbs 18:21New King James Version (NKJV)
[21] **Death and life** *are* **in the power of the tongue, And those who love it will eat its fruit.**

STOP, LISTEN & BREATH:

This section is designed for salient points and takes a ways from what you just read!

Notes:

_____

_____

_____

_____

_____

_____

_____

_____

_____

_____

_____

Chapter 14

Power in Prayer

Philippians 4:6
6 do not be anxious about anything, but in everything by prayer and supplication with thanksgiving let your requests be made known to God.

Praying is the most important thing I need to do in my life before I start my day. I cannot live my life without praying. When I think about my day to day interactions I quickly recognize that my success or lack of success that day is revolved around prayer. I start my day off praying for my family and others. I take pride in going into my sons room and laying my hands on him and saying, Lord watch over him, guide and protect him throughout his day, Lord let no hurt harm or danger come in his dwelling and give him favor. This is a simple prayer that I refuse to leave home without doing. I'm so thankful that God has blessed me with this opportunity to pray for my son and because of this I will not take it for granted that this starts off his day well. Praying this prayer eliminates fears of him being harmed or misused by anyone. I know that God dispatches angels to watch over him because of my prayers. This allows my day to be at peace. I think prayer is just that important.

Oftentimes, I find myself rushing off and forgetting to pray for my day. Once I discover that, I stop by and pray. Prayer prevents the enemy from wining in your life. The bibles states that the enemy is going to and fro in the earth seeking whom to devour. The enemy tries to cause confusion and chaos in the life of every born again believer. Think it not strange that you have mishaps in your day. These mishaps are traps and tricks set by Satan. Christian believers have the same experience however, if you are a believer you have the ability to work through them with a peace of mind. I believe as believers once you read this scripture you should understand the impact that praying daily throughout the day has.

In order to have a productive Christian life one must first understand the importance of praying on a regular daily basis. Prayer cannot and should not be viewed as a daunting task. Talking to your heavenly father about your daily actions and interactions enhances your relationship with God. One simply cannot build a productive relationship with anyone without constant communication. I have heard Christians say I pray all the time but I'm not sure if God is listening to me and my prayers. In praying, it's equally important to know and read God's Holy word. This is a critical part of us gaining understanding of God's various way of communicating. Praying is a very essential part of every Christian's day.

I remember being young in the Lord and reading that the people of God should pray without ceasing and not being able to understand how this is possible unless you lived inside the church and never left out. I have since matured to the full understanding of how to pray without ceasing.

Thessalonians 5:16-18New King James Version (NKJV)
[16] Rejoice always, [17] pray without ceasing, [18] in everything give thanks; for this is the will of God in Christ Jesus for you.

Praying without ceasing doesn't mean you cannot get off your knees from praying or that you have to be in church praying. This simply means you have to have a mindset and an attitude toward prayer. What I mean is that you can pray wherever you are and you don't have to be inside the church. Once your mind and attitude toward prayer shifts to how essential it is to pray without ceasing it becomes natural and part of life.

For example, every day and all day there is always something I petition God for in prayer. I could be going into a meeting and whisper in my mind asking God to please allow this meeting to be productive.

Once inside the meeting. I'm praying to myself asking God to give me the wisdom of how to answer or respond to the questions. Lord, let the people see you in me and not me myself. Lord help me understand what is being said or asked of me. God give me favor in the eyes of man. God I'm not sure how to handle this situation please help me.

This is how your day should be, having a mind to include God in all of your decisions and listen for him to respond. When God responds to us it's not always in the way we would like for him to respond but trust me if you are watching and listening, wait He's always responding and coming to our aid or rescue. The Bible speaks of acknowledging God in all of your ways; we do this by taking the time to consult with God in our daily life decisions.

When it comes right down to it, nothing is more important than talking to Jesus. There is nothing I can do or achieve without God. In my understanding of God's word about my Christian journey I discovered it's a duty to pray. A duty of all born again believers. When we see things going against the will of God according to his word, we should pray. When we look on the news and see the death and destruction that torments our world, we should pray. One of my favorite scriptures in God's Holy Word is 2 Chronicles 7:14

2 Chronicles 7:14New International Version (NIV)
[14] if my people, who are called by my name, will humble themselves and pray and seek my face and turn from their wicked ways, then I will hear from heaven, and I will forgive their sin and will heal their land.

I love this scripture because it gives me hope that no matter the circumstance or situation God is still in total control. Not only is God in control, He has empowered me to be able to make a difference in my life and the life of others. As a child of God, he has empowered me in this scripture when he says if my people who are called by my name. This makes me happy in knowing I am his and I am called by his name. God is speaking about all of his people. God only requires me to humble myself. What that means to me is to recognize who I am and who He is to me. He is Lord over the universe, I am a simple vessel of his handy work. My power is given to me by him so don't be fooled about who is in control, no matter what things may look like always know that God is ultimately in control. For example, perhaps when you were a child and you thought that you were in control of yourself, your mother or father quickly let you know that this is my house, I simply let you live here.

I remember it was this one time my son Christian was a bit angry about having to live up to my expectations when he was about three or four years old. Christian has been taught that it doesn't matter what you see others do, you do what is expected of you. One day, the church was having its annual Labor Day picnic at Enon Park in Chesterfield VA. Christian got into trouble for something he did as he so often did at this age. I really don't even remember what he got into trouble for. Christian shared with his mother that he didn't want to be a Bolar anymore. Niki calls me on the phone and shared with me just what Christian had shared with her.

So, shortly thereafter I arrived home to meet Christian sleeping, or resting comfortable in my bed. I walked around the bed and grab Christian by the hand and we walked calmly down the stairs. Christian never for once asked me where we were going. We made it to the front door and stopped. I said, Christian your mother told me that you said that you did not want to be a Bolar any more. Christian got frightened and responded, yes sir I did say that. Looking terrified, he had been snitched on by his mother. I calmly explained to Christian that this house and everything inside it belong to the Bolars'. I turned the front porch light off and opened the door took Christian by the hand and guided him outside the door where it was dark.

Christian quickly screams with fright "daddy I do want to be Bolar," and I asked him again "are you sure you want to be a Bolar because the Bolar's lived here?" Trying to keep a calm and stern look on my face, I allowed little Christian back into the house. I explained to Christian that I was in charge and if he wanted to live here he needed to understand that, so he agreed. So I asked him the question, "Do you know who is in charge of this house?" He looked at me and humbly said "daddy you are in charge." I asked him "are you sure you want to be a Bolar?" And he said yes.

I know God looks down on us as his children and perhaps laughs at our foolish ways. Often proving to us, I know I have blessed you beyond measure, but I'm still in charge. This information alone humbles me. Then God says, Ok son, Ok daughter know that you have your thoughts together and your attitude has been adjusted now we can talk. In other words, we have to check ourselves. Once we do that, we can share in confidence to God just what's going on and he will hear from heaven and heal our lands.

STOP, LISTEN & BREATH:

This section is designed for salient points and takes a ways from what you just read!

Notes:

_____

_____

_____

_____

_____

_____

_____

_____

_____

Chapter 15

Leading through Gods Lens

> **Proverbs 16:7**
> [7] When a man's ways please the LORD, he makes even his enemies to be at peace with him.

Leading through God's lens is a timely expectation that will focus on the importance of knowing and believing that you are who God said that you are. What exactly does that mean today for the modern day Christian? Is this even possible to do? There are so many questions and so few available answers or so would appear. These are some of the many questions that Christians around the world are seeking answers to. Christians have a tendency to church hop for this very reason. Some church hopers are hopping around because they don't want to stay so they tend to leave. They don't have the discernment needed to make the right decision.

I believe this book will supply some of the basic answers needed to live and lead a productive and successful Christian life. In order to understand leading through God's lens, one must begin with prerequisite. This simply means you cannot begin to comprehend leading through God's lens if you have no knowledge of who God is and his will for our life. This is another important reason to see you through God's lens. There are several necessary components that one must understand and operate within in order to see things though God's lens

The top four are:

1. Salvation
2. Being filled with the Holy Spirit of God
3. A clear understanding of God's word
4. A personal relationship with God.

There are many others that can be added however, seeing through God's lens requires you to have these bare minimum. In my personal experiences of interacting with Christians or perhaps people who have confessed their Christian faith, one or more of these key essential ingredients are missing. I have learned through my personal relationship with God that it's not just to act like a good Christian should. What is meant by this statement is that we can seek to do good and hope that everything works out for our good. This is a sure role of the dice based on my experiences!

What are your thoughts?

_____

_____

_____

_____

_____

_____

_____

Here are my thoughts, as good Christians we can hope for the best but God has given us his word to guide us along this Christian journey. God said in his Holy word that heaven and earth will pass away but, my word will last forever. This simply means that you can take it to the bank, if God said it, it shall come to pass. A bold statement like that along with God saying, I'm not a man that I should lie nor the son of man where I have to repent. This is a very important scripture that every Christian has to take to heart and understand that God's word is just that powerful. Once Christians fully understand the power of what God said in this scripture it validates every scripture. Please read this scripture, study it and take it to heart.

Numbers 23:19 God is not a man, so he does not lie. He is not human, so he does not change his mind. Has he ever spoken and failed to act? Has he ever promised and not carried it through?

What God says is true and should not be taken lightly. We are merely created in God's image and that's wonderful, but make no mistake we are not like God. God is by no way human or subject to the flesh as it is to man. This is very important for you to know because, unless you understand believe and then activate God's word as it is written you cannot have the abundant life. Reason being that you won't be able to stand against the enemy. In fact, you can't even receive what you need from God unless you believe He can.

The other thing is that unless you know God's word and how to use it, it's meaningless and useless to you and for you. On the other hand, if you fully believe in God and affectively use God's word for your life, you simply cannot go wrong. One of my favorite scriptures to focus on when I'm feeling a little fearful, I pull out this scripture. This scripture is so powerful and affects so many areas of fear; you can't help but be brave after quoting it!

Yeah thought I walk through the valley of death ------Psalm 23
David declares, The Lord is my shepherd.

1 The Lord is my shepherd; I shall not want.
2 He maketh me to lie down in green pastures: he leadeth me beside the still waters. 3 He restoreth my soul: he leadeth me in the paths of righteousness for his name's sake. 4 Yea, though I walk through

the valley of the shadow of death, I will fear no evil: for thou art with me; thy rod and thy staff they comfort me. 5 Thou preparest a table before me in the presence of mine enemies: thou anointest my head with oil; my cup runneth over.
6 Surely goodness and mercy shall follow me all the days of my life: and I will dwell in the house of the Lord forever.

If you believe in God and trust his word, how can you read this scripture and operate in fear. This just isn't possible for a true believer. As a believer, we have to focus all of our attention on God and His word to give us the power we need to be brave and confident. God's word has been produced and reproduced in nearly every corner of the earth and in every language for his people's personal use to have life and have it more abundantly. The key is do you believe? I do understand that there are certain trials in life that we go through that are much greater than others but God's word is powerful enough were it still works. As believers, we must take God at his word. I have personally seen God prepare a table before my enemies just as the Holy Scripture says.

I know now that goodness and mercy follow me all the days of my life. There have been things that happened to me where I should have lost but because of God's goodness and mercies following me all the days of my life I end up win. I was trimming my trees one day and the trimmer was slicing tree branches left and right. My arm gave out and out of reflex I reached toward the blade with my left hand and rather than cutting my finger off God protected me, I only received a three small cuts on my finger. This may seem small to you but, I know if God was not with me my entire finger would have been sliced off just like the thick tree branches I had been cutting. I know you may be thinking that I still got cut, true but I didn't lose my finger. When I tell you God is good it's simply because He is. God is so much more than just good he is great and greatly to be praised. There truly is nothing God can't do or want do for his children.

Luke 8:43-45New International Version (NIV)
[43] And a woman was there who had been subject to bleeding for twelve years,[a] but no one could heal her.[44] She came up behind him and touched the edge of his cloak, and immediately her bleeding stopped.[45] "Who touched me?" Jesus asked. When they all denied it, Peter said, "Master, the people are crowding and pressing against you."

In the crowd that day, there was a woman who for twelve years had been afflicted with hemorrhage. She had spent every penny she had on doctors but not even one had been able to help her. She slipped in from behind and touched the edge of Jesus' robe. At that very moment her hemorrhage stopped. Jesus said, "Who touched me?"

When no one stepped forward, Peter said, "But Master, we've got crowds of people on our hands. Dozens have touched you."

1. This touch was out of pure desperation of her faith in Jesus.
2. Although there was a crowd touching Jesus, He knew that this was a special touch that drew virtue out of him.
3. This touch was not gone unnoticed by the savior or her because she was instantly healed by a simple touch of his garment. Not a grab or pull but, a simple touch caused 12 years of suffering to dissipate in a matter of seconds!

This same level of healing is available for all of God's children. I firmly believe one of the main the reasons that healing isn't manifested for all is directly related to their level of faith and desperation. Often time a Christian or non-Christian will be going about life health and hold on until they discover that cancer or some terminal illness has appeared. Once the news hits about the illness, fear with the size of a tsunami comes in. The fear is powerful like a flood. The fear is not like a normal old fear. This fear comes directly from the evil one, Satan. The mission of this fear is designed to kill, steal, and destroy every morsel of hope faith or trust one may have in God. Once this fear creeps in, it begins to break down the immune system that the

Christian automatically inherited by accepting Jesus Christ as their personal savior. The only thing that can prevent the breakdown and stop the destruction of the enemy is the word of God correlated with faith. God's word is bigger than cancer, diabetes, and HIV. The power of God only works when you believe in it. Once the word of God is poured upon your circumstances it instantly starts to combat the tactics of the enemy with a power that is far greater than the enemy can withstand. Listen at these two powerful scriptures that will cause the enemy to flee.

1. No weapon formed against me shall prosper
2. By his stripes I am healed!

These are two of the many scriptures that will save your life. These two scriptures are so powerful, that if you will use them, they will crush the enemy in his tracks. The scriptures without your individual faith can't manifest. Let me explain it like this. God left his word for his people to live, and live an abundant life, however, we have to know the word, speak the word of God, and apply the word of God to release the power that it holds.

In looking closer at the two scriptures, we can see that the power is phenomenal. For example, God's word says, "No weapons formed against me shall prosper." This doesn't mean the weapons won't form or appear. This also does not mean that there won't be any pain or suffering that you feel or experience. What this means is that through it all you will be successful if you believe.

Second scripture, by his stripes you are healed. This means that despite what you may be feeling if you understand the power of God it's already done, and we the children of the highest God have no reason to fear.

Fear is not part of the genetic makeup of the true Christian. As a born again believer of Christ I have no reason to fear. The word of God says it like this; God did not give us a spirit of fear but, of love, power, and a sound mind.

STOP, LISTEN & BREATH:

This section is designed for salient points and takes a ways from what you just read!

    Notes:

_____

_____

_____

_____

_____

_____

_____

_____

_____

_____

_____

_____

_____

Chapter 16

Fivefold Ministry

> **Ephesians 4:12-13**
> 12 qto equip the saints for the work of ministry, for rbuilding up sthe body of Christ, 13 until we all attain to tthe unity of the faith and of the knowledge of the Son of God, uto mature manhood,5 to the measure of the stature of vthe fullness of Christ,

The five-fold ministry to some is still a great mystery to some.

Question: "What is the five (5) fold ministry?"

Answer:

The concept of the five-fold ministry comes from Ephesians 4:11, "It was He who gave some to be (1) apostles, some to be (2) prophets, some to be (3) evangelists, and some to be (4) pastors and (5) teachers." Primarily as a result of this verse, some believe God has restored, or is restoring the offices of apostle and prophet in the church today. Ephesians 4:12-13 tells us that the purpose of the five-fold ministry is, "to prepare God's people for works of service, so that the body of Christ may be built up until we all reach unity in the faith and in the knowledge of the Son of God and become mature, attaining to the whole measure of the fullness of Christ.

"So, since the body of Christ definitely is not built up to unity in the faith and has not attained to the whole measure of the fullness of Christ, the thinking goes, the offices of apostle and prophet must still be in effect. However, Ephesians 2:20 informs us that the church is "built on the foundation of the apostles and prophets, with Christ Jesus

Himself as the chief cornerstone." If the apostles and prophets were the foundation of the church, are we still building the foundation? Hebrews 6:1-3 encourages us to move on from the foundation.

Although, Jesus Christ is most definitely active in the church today, His role as the cornerstone of the church was completed with His death, burial, resurrection, and ascension. If the work of the cornerstone is in that sense complete, so must the work of the apostles and prophets, who were the foundation be complete.

What was the role of the apostles and prophets? It was to proclaim God's revelation, to teach the new truth, the church would need to grow and thrive. The apostles and prophets completed this mission. How, by giving us the Word of God! The Word of God is the completed revelation of God. The Bible contains everything the church needs to know to grow, thrive, and fulfill God's mission (2 Timothy 3:15-16). The cornerstone work of the apostles and prophets is complete. The ongoing work of the apostles and prophets is manifested in the Holy Spirit speaking through and teaching us God's Word. In that sense, the five-fold ministry is still active.

STOP, LISTEN & BREATH:

This section is designed for salient points and takes a ways from what you just read!

Notes:

_____

_____

_____

_____

_____

Chapter 17

Homosexuality

The born again believer, new convert, will face such challenges as to how to understand what road is the right road to follow while on this Christian journey. The church has not historically done a great job on such sensitive topics, like fornication, adultery or homosexuality to the degree it can be stumped out or annulated.

This topic is such a remotely sensitive topic today. I believe it's extremely sensitive for a number of reasons, and factors that I hope to be able to bring some historical meaning and relative understanding that will clear up any misconception that the new or vested Christian can agree and determine on how to create an opportunity that will change lives forever.

To simply not talk about, avoid or to express our views in a dogmatic approach has not provided a clear and precise conceptual understanding to the current over taken or undertaken, that our world or society as we have known it has transformed into. We have witnessed in the last decade a complete take over by the lesbian transgender and gay communities. This massive take over has proven Christians lack of concern, inability to see as seers and lack of power to prevent our world to be balance or ruled by our ability or power given to us by God to hold back the forces of darkness from taking over.

So, what we experience in our society as norms has not always been the case. There is a new world order on this earth and it's designed and led by that old enemy called Satan. However, Satan cannot take credit for this triumphant victory alone. This was designed by him but, there is a much more powerful force working together here. The forces that are teaming up with Satan are the non-believers and the believers. I know you will disagree, I say it is so and here is my rational or belief as to why!

The non-believer stands for very little, and they can and will be swayed by any wind of doctrine. They go off their guts of what's wrong or right or how the world should work, in their eyes or individual belief system. This extremely large body of people often makes decisions that affect our world and lives without any guided principles or connection with a Holy God. Then you have the Christian people who have been so captured by what is happening in their own lives that very little attention is given to the perfecting of the saints.

Saints that have not been perfected by the Word of God and empower by the Holy Spirit, give little or no attention to the world around them, and if they do they are consumed with the little world that revolves around them, and nothing else. This complete lack of attention to what is about to happen before it happens is a strike against the children of God. The bibles says that nothing on this earth shall take place without his prophets knowing about it in advance. Therefore, there should have been an alarm that was sounded, and if the alarm was sounded who heard the sound, and those that heard the sound, how effective they were in sending out the warning. This rage of homosexuality that has taken over, or that has been allowed to run loose on the earth was allowed by God's people

2 Chronicles 7:14-15 14

and My people who are called by My name humble themselves and pray and seek My face and turn from their wicked ways, then I will hear from heaven, will forgive their sin and will heal their land. 15" Now My eyes will be open and My ears attentive to the prayer offered in this place....

The Story Sodom and Gomorrah Destroyed
Genesis 19New International Version (NIV)

19 The two angels arrived at Sodom in the evening, and Lot was sitting in the gateway of the city. When he saw them, he got up to meet them and bowed down with his face to the ground. 2 "My

---

lords," he said, "please turn aside to your servant's house. You can wash your feet and spend the night and then go on your way early in the morning."

"No," they answered, "we will spend the night in the square."

3 But he insisted so strongly that they did go with him and entered his house. He prepared a meal for them, baking bread without yeast, and they ate. 4 Before they had gone to bed, all the men from every part of the city of Sodom—both young and old—surrounded the house.5 They called to Lot, "Where are the men who came to you tonight? Bring them out to us so that we can have sex with them."

6 Lot went outside to meet them and shut the door behind him 7 and said, "No, my friends. Don't do this wicked thing. 8 Look, I have two daughters who have never slept with a man. Let me bring them out to you, and you can do what you like with them. But don't do anything to these men, for they have come under the protection of my roof."

9 "Get out of our way," they replied. "This fellow came here as a foreigner, and now he wants to play the judge! We'll treat you worse than them." They kept bringing pressure on Lot and moved forward to break down the door.

10 But the men inside reached out and pulled Lot back into the house and shut the door.11 Then they struck the men who were at the door of the house, young and old, with blindness so that they could not find the door.

12 The two men said to Lot, "Do you have anyone else here—sons-in-law, sons or daughters, or anyone else in the city who belongs to you? Get them out of here,13 because we are going to destroy this place. The outcry to the Lord against its people is so great that he has sent us to destroy it."

14 So Lot went out and spoke to his sons-in-law, who were pledged to marry[a] his daughters. He said, "Hurry and get out of this place, because the Lord is about to destroy the city!" But his sons-in-law thought he was joking.

15 With the coming of dawn, the angels urged Lot, saying, "Hurry! Take your wife and your two daughters who are here, or you will be swept away when the city is punished."

16 When he hesitated, the men grasped his hand and the hands of his wife and of his two daughters and led them safely out of the city, for the Lord was merciful to them. 17 As soon as they had brought them out, one of them said, "Flee for your lives! Don't look back, and don't stop anywhere in the plain! Flee to the mountains or you will be swept away!"

18 But Lot said to them, "No, my lords,[b]please! 19 Your[c] servant has found favor in your[d] eyes, and you[e] have shown great kindness to me in sparing my life. But I can't flee to the mountains; this disaster will overtake me, and I'll die. 20 Look, here is a town near enough to run to, and it is small. Let me flee to it—it is very small, isn't it? Then my life will be spared."

21 He said to him, "Very well, I will grant this request too; I will not overthrow the town you speak of.22 But flee their quickly, because I cannot do anything until you reach it." (That is why the town was called Zoar.[f])

23 By the time Lot reached Zoar, the sun had risen over the land. 24 Then the Lord rained down burning sulfur on Sodom and Gomorrah—from the Lord out of the heavens. 25 Thus he overthrew those cities and the entire plain, destroying all those living in the cities—and also the vegetation in the land. 26 But Lot's wife looked back, and she became a pillar of salt.

27 Early the next morning Abraham got up and returned to the place where he had stood before the Lord.28 He looked down toward Sodom and Gomorrah, toward all the land of the plain, and he saw dense smoke rising from the land, like smoke from a furnace.

29 So when God destroyed the cities of the plain, he remembered Abraham, and he brought Lot out of the catastrophe that overthrew the cities where Lot had lived.

What was the sin of Sodom according to Genesis 19?

The text of Genesis 19 implies that even though Lot made an offer of his virgin daughters to be raped, his offer was refused by the men of this city. God apparently had a fierce anger directed at the other inhabitants of the town. He destroyed Sodom with fire and brimstone (sulfur) dumped from above. According to the story, he killed all of the men and women of Sodom, as well as all the innocent children, infants, newborns, etc. who lived in the city.

It is clear from this brief passage in Genesis why God demolished the city.

The following theories and research on this topic have been advanced.

The people of Sodom:

1. **Engaged in consensual homosexual acts** -- a same-sex orgy in this case. This is the belief of the most conservative Christians. This option seems unlikely because:
   - Genesis 19:5 said that *all* of the men (perhaps all of the people) of Sodom formed the mob at Lot's house and demanded to "know" the angels. The percentage of homosexuals in a typical group of male adults is generally around 5%, not 100%.

   - Finally, as noted above, if the men of Sodom were all homosexuals, there would be few if any children and widows in the city are mentioned elsewhere in the Bible.

2. **Were uncharitable and abusive to strangers**, the poor, sick, and disadvantaged. In that society, a person had a very strong obligation to protect any guests in their home. Many liberal Christians believe that this is the meaning behind the story of the destruction of Sodom. This belief has considerable support in the many other references to Sodom in the Bible and Jewish literature.

3. **Wanted to humiliate their visitors** by engaging in "*an act of sexual degradation and male rape... These are acts of violence*

that are committed by parties seeking to show their hatred for those they are degrading. It is not an act of love or of caring" **1** some theologians suggests that the sin of Sodom was the threat of mass rape.

4. **Wanted to engage in bestiality** -- having sex with members of another species. The mob may have wanted to rape the angels; angels are not human beings rather they are of a different species. This would be consistent with the frequently mistranslated verse in Jude about the men of Sodom going after *"other flesh"* or *"strange flesh."*

5. **Wanted to absorb the power of the angels:** In ancient times, sacred sex was very common. People would engage in sexual intercourse with temple prostitutes who represented a god or goddess. By doing so, the people believed that they would receive a blessing from their deity. If the people of Sodom realized that angels sent by God were present in their city, the men of Sodom may have concluded that raping the angels might give them supernatural powers.

What were the sins of Sodom according to other biblical passages that refer to the city?
A common procedure in biblical apologetics is to let the Bible interpret itself. Looking elsewhere in the Bible for references to Sodom may help us determine which of the four above interpretations is correct.
The interpretation of Genesis 19 as referring to a homosexual sin appears to have been created in the 11th century by the Italian ascetic St. Peter Damian. 3 Christian theologians generally accepted this explanation until recently. In fact, the English word *sodomy,* **which popularly means** *either homosexual or heterosexual anal intercourse,* **was derived from the name of the city. The term "sodomy" is also used in some ancient laws to refer to a variety of sexual behaviors in addition to heterosexual intercourse.**

Ezekeiel 16:49-50:*"Now this was the sin of your sister Sodom: She and her daughters were arrogant, overfed and unconcerned; they did not help the poor and needy. They were haughty and did detestable things before me. Therefore I did away with them as you have seen."* **God states clearly that he destroyed Sodom's sins because of their pride, their excess of food while the poor and needy suffered; sexual activity is not even mentioned.**

Matthew 10:14-15: Jesus implied that the sin of the people of Sodom was to be inhospitable to strangers.

Luke 10:7-16: This is parallel passage to the verses from Matthew.

2 Peter 6-8: Peter mentions that God destroyed the adults and children of Sodom because the former were ungodly, unprincipled and lawless.

Jude, Verse 7: Jude wrote that Sodom's sins were sexual in nature. Various biblical translations of this passage in Jude describes the sin as: *fornication, going after strange flesh, sexual immorality, perverted sensuality, homosexuality, lust of every kind, immoral acts* and *unnatural lust*. It looks as if the translators were unclear of the meaning of the verse in its original Greek, and simply selected their favorite sin to attack. The original Greek is transliterated as: *"sarkos heteras."* This can be translated as *"other flesh."* Ironically, our English word *"heterosexual"* comes from *"heteras."*

A likely interpretation is that the author of Jude **4** criticized the men of Sodom for wanting to engage in sexual activities with angels. Angels are described in the Bible as a species of created beings who were different from humans. The sin of the people of Sodom would be that of bestiality. Another possibility is that the *"other flesh"* refers to cannibalism, which was a practice associated with early Canaanite culture. However, there is no mention in Genesis 19 about actually eating the angels. **On the other hand there are some passages which might imply that the sin of Sodom was homosexuality:**

Jeremiah 49:18: Some conservative theologians have interpreted this verse as criticizing the inhabitants of Jerusalem for their sexual sins, and implying that they were like the men of Sodom.

Ezekeiel 16:50: Although the preceding verse describes Sodom's sins as pride, laziness, insensitivity to the needs of the poor, and haughtiness, verse 50 refers to the citizens of Sodom as having *"committed abomination."* The Hebrew word *"to'ebah,"* translated here as *"abomination,"* was used throughout the Hebrew Scriptures (Old Testament) to refer to various ritually impure acts, such as Hebrews and Egyptians eating together, Hebrews eating lobster, shrimp, or snakes, sacrificing an animal in the temple that contained a blemish, women wearing men's clothing (e.g. pants), a man remarrying his former wife, etc. It was also used in **Leviticus 18:22 and 20:13** to condemn same-sex activity between two males. It is not known which "abomination(s)" occurred in Sodom, but it could conceivably have been same-gender sexual activity.

STOP, LISTEN & BREATH:

This section is designed for salient points and takes a ways from what you just read!

Notes:

_____

_____

_____

_____

_____

_____

Bishop Stacey M. Roberts

Biographical Information

Bishop Stacey M. Roberts is a Virginia Native and Senior Pastor of Macedonia Tabernacle Ministries. His personal proverb and mission of the church is "Striving for Excellence in Our Spiritual Walk" in every area of our lives. He believes in the development of the whole man, which is the spirit, soul, and body. He has experienced many miracles of God, but the greatest one is when Jesus saved and delivered him from sin. Bishop Roberts has created a house of worship were the atmosphere of freedom sets those held captive by their circumstance free. Bishop Roberts started his journey in Christ at a young age and gave his life to the Lord in 1981. During his early years, he served as Deacon of a local church and as a minister of the Lord when he was later called to preach the gospel of Jesus Christ. In 1984, he began to travel to various foreign mission trips including Haiti, Canada, and London. But Haiti has profoundly remained in his heart, and he has traveled several times to preach and help the people there. In, 1985, Bishop Roberts was ordained as the Associate Minister at Calvary Pentecostal Tabernacle, Richmond VA. In 1987, he was consecrated as a Bishop in the Full Gospel Tabernacle Bronx, New York and was later elected to serve as Vice-President of the Full Gospel Tabernacle Bronx, New York for seven years.

In 1989, he became the overseeing Bishop over several churches in Toronto, Canada. In 1990, Bishop Roberts was ordained as the Pastor of Oak Grove Baptist Church in Chesterfield, VA where he vitalized the congregation to bring youth back to the church. In 1995, he was elected to serve as the Administrative Bishop in the Full Gospel Tabernacle in Bronx, New York. He later became an Elder of the Morris Cerrullo World Wide Evangelism Ministry. On June 2, 2000, he resigned from being the pastor of Oak Grove Baptist and re-established Macedonia Tabernacle Ministries through the word of prophecy from the Lord.

Bishop Roberts is used by God in a way that cannot be explained, God uses him in the Gifts of the Spirit, the gift of healing, and prophecy. The Holy Spirit gives him prophetic songs in which lives are completely changed. This is just a portion of what God is doing in his life.

Leadership Style

As a leader of this miracle house, God has appointed me to carry out his vision for the last days, along with many other leaders in the Kingdom of Christ. My leadership style in the Kingdom of Christ is that of a visionary leader, with the heart of God to do the work of the Lord. As a visionary leader, God has provided me with an insight, wisdom, and visionary plans that depicts a crystal-clear picture in the direction that the Lord has ordained for my calling, and appointment in these last days. As a visionary leader, God has ordained me to carry out his vision and make the vision of the Lord transferrable to others within the ministry in order to create unity in God's visions and plans.

The gift of walking, and leading in God's visionary plan, allows leaders like me to cast powerful visions, and indefatigable enthusiasm to pursue the mission of Christ. Visionaries shamelessly appeal to anyone and everyone to motivate people to get on board with the vision. The people become inflamed and ignited with the vision and begin to share in the plans of the Lord up to the point where everyone talks about it, write about it, and burn red hot for it. Visionary leaders are future oriented, spiritually idealistic, and full of faith in order to believe that the vision can and will be actualized.

Visionary mindsets foster realistic manifestations of God given plans and dreams that are cast to others through faith talking. Visionary leaders are not easily discouraged or deterred. In fact, if people tell leaders like myself that their dreams are impossible, that just adds fuel to the fire in their spirit and propels their dream to grow more. Doubt from others does not cause the vision to cease. The vision gets carried on and cast to others that will draw people into the vision. Many hold on to the vision for an eternity, past the earthly realm like Moses. Visionary leaders have the God given ability to break an exciting vision into achievable steps so that an organization can march intentionally toward the actualization of their mission.

Spiritual Encounters

I have had many spiritual encounters in Christ. As a young babe in Christ, I was on a journey for the spiritual things of Christ. I have been to places like Calvary Church, in Ashland, Virginia, where I have been exposed to many spiritual encounters with Christ. I have been to other healing ministries, such as Benny Henn, and have witnessed the manifestation of God. I have experienced God's glory, interactions with angels, and miracles from God and physical manifestation from God's presence. I have had many heavenly spiritual encounters. My most memorable spiritual encounters are the encounters where you witness the demonic activity in the spirit realm being defeated and bound by God's angels.

I remember being on the mission field in Haiti, where the demonic activity is very strong and the evidence of this is demonstrated physically. Many people on this mission field did not want to eat a certain fish because the people believed that the big sized fish were babies and children. These Haitians would rather eat tiny size fish rather than purchase a fish that could feed a family. These people were bound by witchcraft and demonic practices. I witnessed the physical and spiritual manifestation of people being freed by angels through the preaching and teaching of the gospel, where their faith was increased to withstand the whiles of the devil.

Five favorite Scriptures

1. Luke 6:19 TLV Everyone in the crowd was trying to touch Him, because power flowed from Him, and He was healing them all.

This is one of my favorite Bible verses because Jesus did not need to touch them; they touched him and were healed because the power of the Holy Spirit, which is like a wind or energy, flowed out of him into them.

2. 2 Corinthians 4:4 AMPC For the god of this world has blinded the unbelievers' minds [that they should not discern the truth],

preventing them from seeing the illuminating light of the Gospel of the glory of Christ (the Messiah), who is the Image and Likeness of God.

This is one of my favorite Bible verses because many of the things that we believe for and pray about, in this world that Satan is god of, are able to come to pass in this satanic world through God's power to manifest His promises to His people.

3. Acts 27:10 AMPC Saying, Sirs, I perceive [after careful observation] that this voyage will be attended with disaster and much heavy loss, not only of the cargo and the ship but of our lives, also.

This is one of my favorite bible verses because the scripture resonates with me in how we need perception in the spirit in life; we need to pay attention to the spirit of God.

4. 1Timothy 6:12 AMPC Fight the good fight of the faith; lay hold of the eternal life to which you were summoned and [for which] you confessed the good confession [of faith] before many witnesses.

It is important to fight to maintain a good report of faith. It is not easy to do so when the giants of life are standing there to stop you, by looking like a grasshopper in their sight. Therefore, fight the good fight of faith in order to be an over comer.

5. Mark 11: 24 AMPC For this reason I am telling you, whatever you ask for in prayer, believe trust and be confident) that it is granted to you, and you will [get it].

Be sincere in the things that you desire when you pray so that you will receive the desires of your heart. When you are praying for others, that person has to desire, as well, which is having faith in what they are asking for.

Greatest Challenge

As a leader in the Army of God, I have been confronted with many challenges, naturally and spiritually in life. One of my greatest challenges was on June 2, 2000, when God was transitioning me into a leadership role from one place of worship to another. In the 90's, God sent me to a Baptist church to minister and lead; after many years on the mission field and in various Pentecostal and Apostolic Ministries. I obeyed God and did the will of God through service and leadership for ten years at this Baptist Church. During this period of time, God was reviving many things within this dry place. God had a plan. The last couple of years, I began to have to fight witchcraft within the church committed by some people within this Baptist Church. Unnatural things began to happen to me and my family. The devil was not happy with the spiritual rebirth within this Baptist church and began to plot. One Sunday morning, my family and I went to this Baptist Church to find that I was locked out of the church, along with other church members, by some church officials. By the grace of God and His divine plan to set his people free and deliver the members from this oppressive, religious bondage. At this point and time, the devil was exposed to the members that desired spiritual things from God, what I had been fighting for the past few years prior to June 2, 2000. God gave me a divine plan to set these people free and not leave them in bondage in this Baptist Church, with the other members that did not desire spirituality and the deeper things of God. We left the bondage, and God allowed me to rebirth Macedonia Tabernacle Ministries, with those who desired the spiritual things of God. We began worshiping at a house in the summer of 2000. Then in the fall of 2000, we began to worship in a school. We continued to worship in a school until mid-year 2003. In 2003, God blessed our ministry with a building. I and the members were able to receive the promises of God. When we left the Baptist church, we did not take anything with us, we left everything, all finances, and physical assets. God truly has blessed us and has been able to sustain us with every need that I and the ministry has had. We have been blessed at Macedonia Tabernacle Ministries, since its rebirth on June 2, 2000.

Why I should Follow Jesus

Choosing to follow Jesus is a choice that you will make through time, by allowing God's sovereign will to take charge of your life. All I can do is introduce you to Christ, by telling you who he has been to me, and by allowing my relationship with Christ to shine bright through my life. I can say that you should follow Jesus because he is the greatest. He is the one, true, living God. There are many imitators and imposters that claim to be able to duplicate the same results of eternal life. But there is only one God who has overcame death. I can say all these things, in an effort to convince you, but what I will do is introduce you to God's word in the Bible. Don't read God's word like a fairy tale, or science fiction book, don't turn to the fog of information found on Google or social media sites. Read the word, the Bible for yourself as a primary resource. Personally, reading the Bible, will ensure that the information you need is received directly by you and not lost in translation through the obscurity of Google messages, scriptures, or sermons that aren't validated by accounts, testimonies and witnesses from first hand observers and participants, like Matthew, Mark, Luke and John. The Bible has been validated, signed, sealed and delivered to anyone that desires salvation through the Holy Spirit. I have introduced you to God by giving you his diary, the Bible. Reading the Bible for yourself provides you with the opportunity to gain access to the keys of the Kingdom and experiencing Jesus. When you experience Jesus and have an encounter with Him, you will want to follow him from now until eternity; forever nurturing your relationship with your Lord and Savior Jesus Christ.

By
Bishop Stacey M. Roberts

Debra Underwood

June 2013: Life was good, had a job with little stress most of the time, it was rewarding to me as well as my patients and their family members. To be able to wittiness of God's Mercy and Grace, comforting the family during the transition, however, I was emotional at times. My husband had a Dr's appointment, I usually go with him, we have the same primary care doctor, and I had worked with him over the years. When the visit was about to end, God spoke to me to mention the lump in my breast, I had noticed it for over a year prior to this date, but I was so trying to help everyone else get their lives together so I just put that aside, being a nurse for so many years I knew it needed to be addressed sooner. He immediately wrote orders for a mammogram; I had a lump removed from the same breast years before. When I received the results of the biopsy, they ordered I had only shared it with my husband (the lump), and I reassured him it was alright.

Upon receiving the results of the biopsy, I became very concerned. I decided not to tell friends, just my husband and children, I really prayed for strength to tell them, I couldn't allow them to see that I had any fear or real concern in this matter, I couldn't let them see me weak when I told them. They all were concern, and showed little emotion, that was good for me.

The plan was

1. surgery for a partial mastectomy

2. 4 rounds of chemo

3. 33 rounds of radiation therapy

One week later, a second surgery was necessary, test showed the cancerous cells where still present. I was feeling as though no one really cared, because everyone was so busy doing, they didn't take time out to come by or even call. But I was ok. In August, I started radiation treatments, after the first treatment, I said this is a breeze, but little did I know, after a couple weeks of everyday treatments, I started to notice I was not walking as fast and I became more fatigued as time went on because I was quickly becoming more and more tired. During the treatments, I got the shingle virus, that was very painful, but it was resolved quickly, praise God.

October 24th first chemo treatment, I was concerned about how I was going to react to the treatments and the side effects. The first side effect was blisters in every mucus membrane and nausea, and I wasn't just not feeling well, wanting to just lay down in a fetal position and not move. This feeling lasted until a few days before the next treatment, my husband was there helping in every way possible, although he worked overnight he made sure my needs were met, but even with that there were days that I felt so lonely, nobody had time for me, I was alone and when I needed something to eat, or drink, there was no one there with me but, God was there. Even in times when my husband was home I felt alone, often I thought of my mother, if only she was here. On those days when I was so sick, no one would call or come by or just check on me. No family friends no one. I reminded myself that I would never neglect them that way, how could they not love me, with all the sacrifices I've made for them.

CHEMOBRAIN:

In the middle of a conversation, my mind would just go blank, I could not remember what we were talking about, in the middle of a task I'd just forget what I was doing, and it was a challenge to cook recipes I've known for years. I couldn't remember, I had to read, something 4 or 5 times because I would forget what I just read, most nights I slept only 2 hours no matter what I took for sleep. Neuropathy: pain in my feet, hands, burning tingling, reduced sensation of touch, poor, balance, weakness, cramping muscle, slow reflexes, limping. Changes in appetite, foods you love you don't want, water doesn't have a good taste. Insentience of bladder, and sometimes bowl, so if you go anywhere you have to be prepared, I chose to stay home most of the time for that reason, whenever I did it was necessary for me to know a day in advance, to remember all getting ready entailed for me.

Most people think all this changes immediately after your last treatments are completed, but they don't. It's important to exercise and diet is important. A strong support system is also important, most importantly in having a right relationship with Christ. I sought the Lord in a way I never had before, my favor scriptures are the ones I memorized, and quoted daily, when in pain or any situation. The battle with cancer is real, it changes your whole life mentally, physically, spiritually and emotionally, knowing Christ and that HE will do just what HE said HE will do, cancer don't stand a chance. HE's bigger than cancer.

MY MIRACULOUS SPIRITUAL ENCOUNTERS

July 1981; I didn't know the Lord, I heard about Him but no one ever really told me of Him, the things I had endured in the past,and being around church going people you would think someone would have taken time to introduce you, I just thought may be God only loved certain people. I did attend a Catholic school, attended church, but I never knew what they were saying, and I wasn't about to confess anything.

One day something came up with a close family member, mom and I panicked as we always did, tried everything we could to help, nothing happened, and the burden was very heavy. While just sitting around crying, because you have done all you can, I ignored all the urges I had to pray, after the children were settled and the house was quiet, I got down on my knees, and began to pray, but only for my family member. At some point, I started to confess that I didn't know how to pray, I ask the Lord to help me to pray for him, immediately I started praying scriptures I had never read or heard of before, these are the scriptures in the order HE gave them to me: Psalm 51:10 Create in me a clean heart, O God; and renew in me a right spirit within me; 51:2 wash me thoroughly from my iniquity, and cleanse me from my sin. 51:4 Against thee, and thee only, have I sinned, and done evil in thy sight: I had my eyes closed the whole time, but then I could sense someone was kneeling on the left side of me,and someone directly standing behind me, I started to hear the left side shouting, "get up, open your eyes, get up" but the one behind me very calmly said "No don't open your eyes, don't get up, just keep praying" and I kept praying, I think I was saying the same scriptures over and over again, after sometime, suddenly, I literally felt something or someone come out of me and walked away. I remember that experience like it was yesterday, I will never forget. It has taken many trails, tribulations, and challenges in my life to really get to know the Lord as I now do; I know personally that HE is Real.

MY 5 of FAVORITE SCRIPTURES AND WHY:

Matthew 11:29 "take my yoke upon you, and learn of me, I am meek and lowly in heart, and ye shall find rest unto your souls". Reason: Realizing that only God could make everything in my life right. Isaiah 54:17 "No weapon formed against me shall prosper, and ever tongue that rise up against thee in judgment salt be condemned.... This is the heritage of the servants of the Lord, and their righteousness is of me saith the Lord". REASON: Knowing that it does not matter what the enemy plans to hurt me, it will not prosper, it may form but it will not prosper. Philippians 4:6-7 "Be careful for nothing; but in everything by prayer and supplication with thanksgiving let your request be made known unto God. And the peace of God which passeth all understanding shall keep your hearts and your mines through Christ Jesus".

REASON:
I know that God is my source and my only source, I can tell HIM all about my struggles, and HE will fix it in a way that is best for me. Philippians 4:8 "Finally my brethren, whatsoever things that are true, whatsoever things are honest, whatsoever things are just, whatsoever things are pure, whatsoever things are lovely, whatsoever things are of good report". REASON: Thinking on the "goodness" of God, you immediately rebuke the enemy, focus on the positive stay away from the negative, take on a new mindset.

The Cancer Journey:

Receiving a diagnosis of cancer is never easy, it doesn't sink in right away. When the doctor was explaining about the report, and the plan, I could hear him, but couldn't comprehend what he was saying at the time, the initial shock, unbelief followed by a period of distress, characterized by mixed symptoms of anxiety, and depression, sadness, insomnia, difficulty concentrating.

After telling my family brought some relief, along with their acceptance, and encouragement. All the uncertainty of my well-being, and what am I going to do if things went bad. Sadness and depression had set in so strongly that I didn't have the strength to get out of bed to even take shower, after a few days I said to myself, enough, this is not God's will, but there is something missing, I started searching the scripture, "Genesis 15:6 (LB version) "Abram believed God; then God considered him righteous on account of his faith". Maybe my faith wasn't strong enough, I know I had a right relationship with God, but there is something else God wants me to know, so I continued to search the scriptures, how could I get the faith of Abraham, I believed Gods word, I had to be sure I fully understood being righteous before God, Proverbs 21:21(LB version) "The man who tries to be good, loving, and kind finds life, righteousness and honor". Matthew 6:33 (LB version) "But seek first His Kingdom, and His righteousness, and all these things will be given to you as well", the more I searched the word the more God gave me revelation and the closer I came to Him. Over a period of time of searching the word, I was lead to Mark 11:22-23 (LB version) "Jesus said to His disciples, "If you only have faith in God, you can say to this mountain 'rise up and fall into the sea', and your command will be obeyed.

All that is required is that you really believe and have no doubt! Listen to me! You can pray for anything, and if you believe, you have it; it's yours! But, when you pray forgive anyone your holding a grudge against, so your Father in Heaven will forgive you your sins too." I followed instructions, prayed about my condition, and then God gave me Psalms 91:16 "Long life will I satisfy him (you) and show him (you) His salvation." If it had not been for the Lord on my side, where would I

---

be, Praise God I made it. Whenever things seem rough and I feel I can't go on, or when the pain gets unbearable I quote theses scriptures over and over until it stops, and goes away.

By
Debra Underwood

Rev. Dr. Shawn Scott

I am Rev. Dr. Shawn Scott, my leadership style consists of a combination and orator style. I'm a native of Brooklyn N.Y. My parents are Annie & the late Walter Ross. I am the youngest of six brothers and one sister. My extended family is Mr. & Mrs. Leon Harris and family. I received my Bachelors of Christian Counseling, Honorary Doctorate of Divinity, Master of Divinity, and Doctorate of Christian Education from Higher Learning Bible Institute International Seminary.

I work as an Anesthesia Tech Supervisor of Henrico Doctors Forest Campus Hospital. God has blessed me to have amazing mentors in my life, the late Bishop Melvin Scott of Washington N.C., Dr. Barbara Taylor-Harris of Richmond, VA, Rev. Kenneth Shepherd of Richmond, VA, and Rev. Maynard Jones of Avonia, VA. I am the senior pastor of Ridgeway Baptist Church in Scottsville, VA. My greatest joy is being married to my queen, Mary Scott. Our happiness has been made complete sharing as the proud parents of our two son's Javiell Scott and Ja'Bril Scott. I am also the lead singer of the Fantastic Goldenaires gospel group of Richmond, VA. I'm a preacher through the help of the Holy Spirit that can reach all listeners, children, and adults. God gives me power for whatever audience there is to reach and change lives.

Our bible encourages men, women, boys, and girls to have a vision. God had the most miraculous vision of the universe. God saw it in a vision, God spoke it in order to come too reality, then God made it happen. God blessed me to have a vision to reach our youths not only in the church but, their friends and in the community. We have a Community Day at my church with a lot of fun activities for all ages. I believe we have to get to know our youths, this day in time there is a lot of peer pressure. Too often our youth can feel invisible as if they don't have a voice to be heard. We have to let them know that we are here for them through the wonderful and even the unacceptable times. God will show us a vision which is similar to dreams; this is a gift from God. In Isaiah 1:1 The vision of Isaiah the son of Amos which he saw concerning Judah and Jerusalem in the days of Uzziah, Jotham, Ahaz, and Hezekiah, Kings of Judah. Cultivating a relationship with the Holy Spirit and the understanding of the supernatural is an exciting part of our spiritual journey. Because of this perspective we are able to open our hearts to the possibilities of miracles, signs, and wonders. Miracles occur when the impossible becomes a reality. These things still happen and more amazingly, the Holy Spirit lives in us. We want to be wise and discerning so we can recognize when something is godly and when something is ungodly. We want to demonstrate the true power of God's spirit so others can know him and experience his wonders also.

Favorite Scriptures

Psalm 121: 7-8 (Life)
The lord will keep you from all harm he will watch over your life; the lord will watch over your coming and going both now and forevermore.

Understand that at every moment, God is watching over us. Even in times of suffering and adversity God is safe keeping us even though we are experiencing difficulties.

Proverbs 16:3 (planning)
Commit to the Lord whatever you do and he will establish your plans.

If we completely depend upon God in our work, God will originate our plans. God will bring to pass our plans. We can believe God to bring our work to completion in God's time. When our planning aligns with God's word success will follow.

1 Peter 5:6 (humility)
Humble yourselves, therefore under God's mighty hand, that he may lift you up in due time

Humility will only with stand in the presence of God. When God is not in the mist there is no humility. In this stratosphere humility cannot survive It disappears with God. When we neglect God, we began to place in the atmosphere hostile humility.

Colossians 4: 5-6 (Wisdom)
Be wise in the way you act toward outsiders, make the most of every opportunity. Let your conversation be always full of grace, seasoned with salt, so that you may know how to answer everyone.

There are some believers and some unbelievers. We must be wise in our behavior to those who are outside. In Genesis 6, there were the eight insiders in the ark and then there were the outsiders. On the Day of Judgment day there will be saints and sinners. Then we have the ones who are welcomed into the heavenly kingdom and on the other side we have those who are cast off into the fiery pits of hell. Our words can have a major effect on people when we speak, our words can help an unbeliever believe in God and want to know about the great man we speak about. When people come into the house of the Lord, your first impression should be your best to help them understand the Christian journey. Be wise in the way we act when we are being seen and heard by the unbelievers or anyone else.

Ephesians 6: 1-4 (honor)
Children, obey your parents in the lord for this is right. Honor thy father and mother, which is the first commandment with promise: That it may be well with thee, and thou mayest live long on the earth. And ye fathers, provoke not your children to wrath, but bring them up in the nurture and admonition of the lord.

Young children do not have the comprehension to make judgments based on rationalizing things out and acting in their best interests. We as parents are instructed in our rolls to guide our children to have a personal relationship with God. Most times what a child sees in their parents will have a huge impact on their life. Yes it starts at home where we teach our children to honor, respect, and how to have the love for God and a strong church family.

I am a very spiritual person. I communicate with God constantly through fasting, praying, reading my bible, and singing. I always turn to God when faced with challenges in my life. We all have challenges such as personal life, work, family or friends, it can be any situation.

In my early 20's, I was always pushing the ministry to the back of my mind. I knew I had a calling on my life but, I was just not prepared to answer the call. I would say to myself what would my friends or family say. As years went by, it finally hit me that if I can deny my calling it's like I'm denying God. The older you get the more mature and wiser you become. That day I had a long talk with God while driving, I told God, I will not deny my calling, it's all about you God not me. I thank God each and every day that God never left me. In life there are choices, we live and learn from our choices we make. My wife and I always tell our son's when circumstances happen from the choices you make it is a learning experience. I myself personally had to learn that growing up. Therefore, I'm so blessed that what God has planted in me I am able to help others and guide them the way God has help to place me where I am today. It was a challenge and hard work with school, work, family, but God showed me how to balance my life. We have to learn how to balance life through it all; it will work out for the good of the Lord. I am certainly a witness. Proverbs 16:11 A just weight and balance are the Lord's all the weights of the bag are His work.

Why Choose Christ

Everyone is following someone or something, so, I would say why not try following Jesus. John 8:12 then spoke Jesus again unto them saying, I am the light of the world: he that follows me shall not walk in darkness, but shall have the light of life. Jesus will never leave you nor for sake you. He will be with you through good, and bad. We can always count on Jesus when we tell him about our situations we don't have to worry about it being broadcast to the next person.

Jesus will be there to wipe our tears away, and whisper in our ears to say my child don't give up now, you have come too far just to throw in the towel. Jesus is saying I am here, all you have to do is read your bible I have all the answers. Why not follow Jesus to the path of righteousness?

By
Rev. Dr. Shawn Scott

Chapter 18

The principles of God

The word of God is much underutilized in the day to day life of the Christian believer. Jesus distinctly said, He came that we may have life, and have life more abundantly. The abundance is not all about houses, cars or land but, more about a balance life filled with peace, good health, love for all mankind, and honoring and acknowledging God in all of our ways. These are attributes of a health and whole life that honor, and please God in a way that is not common to man, in the age that we live in today. In fact, we are living in a modern day sodom and Gomorra time.

God's

God's Word contains literally thousands of Bible promises waiting to be claimed in faith. Below we've listed just a few. It's our prayer that your faith, and trust in our Heavenly Father will be increased as you seek Him to supply your every need. May you be blessed?

(NOTE: All Scripture references are from the KJV Bible)

Addictions | Deliverance from demonic harassment | Depression | Family | Fear | Filling of Holy Spirit Finances / Jobs | Forgiveness | Guidance | Health | Marriage / Companionship | Salvation / God's Love | Strength to do God's will

Addictions

And call upon me in the day of trouble: I will deliver thee, and thou shalt glorify me.
- Psalms 50:15

Is not this the fast that I have chosen? to loose the bands of wickedness, to undo the heavy burdens, and to let the oppressed go free, and that ye break every yoke?
- Isaiah 58:6

The Spirit of the Lord GOD is upon me; because the LORD hath anointed me to preach good tidings unto the meek; he hath sent me to bind up the brokenhearted, to proclaim liberty to the captives, and the opening of the prison to them that are bound;
- Isaiah 61:1

If the Son therefore shall make you free, ye shall be free indeed.
- John 8:36

There is therefore now no condemnation to them which are in Christ Jesus, who walk not after the flesh, but after the Spirit.
- Romans 8:1

There hath no temptation taken you but such as is common to man: but God is faithful, who will not suffer you to be tempted above that ye are able; but will with the temptation also make a way to escape, that ye may be able to bear it.
- 1 Corinthians 10:13

Therefore if any man be in Christ, he is a new creature: old things are passed away; behold, all things are become new.
- 2 Corinthians 5:17

This I say then, Walk in the Spirit, and ye shall not fulfil the lust of the flesh.
- Galatians 5:16

Deliverance from demonic harassment

The angel of the LORD encampeth round about them that fear him, and delivereth them.
- Psalms 34:7

For thou hast been a shelter for me, and a strong tower from the enemy.
- Psalms 61:3

Because he hath set his love upon me, therefore will I deliver him: I will set him on high, because he hath known my name.
- Psalms 91:14

And Jesus said unto them, Because of your unbelief: for verily I say unto you, If ye have faith as a grain of mustard seed, ye shall say unto this mountain, Remove hence to yonder place; and it shall remove; and nothing shall be impossible unto you.
- Matthew 17:20

The Spirit of the Lord is upon me, because he hath anointed me to preach the gospel to the poor; he hath sent me to heal the brokenhearted, to preach deliverance to the captives, and recovering of sight to the blind, to set at liberty them that are bruised,
- Luke 4:18

Submit yourselves therefore to God. Resist the devil, and he will flee from you.
- James 4:7

And I heard a loud voice saying in heaven, Now is come salvation, and strength, and the kingdom of our God, and the power of his Christ: for the accuser of our brethren is cast down, which accused them before our God day and night.
- Revelation 12:10

Depression

The LORD also will be a refuge for the oppressed, a refuge in times of trouble.
- Psalms 9:9

The righteous cry, and the LORD heareth, and delivereth them out of all their troubles.
- Psalms 34:17

Then they cried unto the LORD in their trouble, and he saved them out of their distresses.
- Psalms 107:13

Heaviness in the heart of man maketh it stoop: but a good word maketh it glad.
- Proverbs 12:25

Fear thou not; for I am with thee: be not dismayed; for I am thy God: I will strengthen thee; yea, I will help thee; yea, I will uphold thee with the right hand of my righteousness.
- Isaiah 41:10

For the mountains shall depart, and the hills be removed; but my kindness shall not depart from thee, neither shall the covenant of my peace be removed, saith the LORD that hath mercy on thee.
- Isaiah 54:10

It is of the LORD's mercies that we are not consumed, because his compassions fail not. They are new every morning: great is thy faithfulness.
- Lamentations 3:22-23

Family

Honour thy father and thy mother: that thy days may be long upon the land which the LORD thy God giveth thee.
- Exodus 20:12

But the mercy of the LORD is from everlasting to everlasting upon them that fear him, and his righteousness unto children's children;
- Psalms 103:17

Train up a child in the way he should go: and when he is old, he will not depart from it.
- Proverbs 22:6

The father of the righteous shall greatly rejoice: and he that begetteth a wise child shall have joy of him.
- Proverbs 23:24

For I will pour water upon him that is thirsty, and floods upon the dry ground: I will pour my spirit upon thy seed, and my blessing upon thine offspring:
- Isaiah 44:3

But thus saith the LORD, Even the captives of the mighty shall be taken away, and the prey of the terrible shall be delivered: for I will contend with him that contendeth with thee, and I will save thy children.
- Isaiah 49:25

And he shall turn the heart of the fathers to the children, and the heart of the children to their fathers...
- Malachi 4:6

Fear

The LORD shall fight for you, and ye shall hold your peace.
- Exodus 14:14

And the LORD, he it is that doth go before thee; he will be with thee, he will not fail thee, neither forsake thee: fear not, neither be dismayed.
- Deuteronomy 31:8

I will call upon the LORD, who is worthy to be praised: so shall I be saved from mine enemies.
- Psalms 18:3

Yea, though I walk through the valley of the shadow of death, I will fear no evil: for thou art with me; thy rod and thy staff they comfort me.
- Psalms 23:4

The LORD is my light and my salvation; whom shall I fear? the LORD is the strength of my life; of whom shall I be afraid?
- Psalms 27:1

For I the LORD thy God will hold thy right hand, saying unto thee, Fear not; I will help thee.
- Isaiah 41:13

When thou passest through the waters, I will be with thee; and through the rivers, they shall not overflow thee: when thou walkest through the fire, thou shalt not be burned; neither shall the flame kindle upon thee.
- Isaiah 43:2

Peace I leave with you, my peace I give unto you: not as the world giveth, give I unto you. Let not your heart be troubled, neither let it be afraid.
- John 14:27

Filling of Holy Spirit

Turn you at my reproof: behold, I will pour out my spirit unto you, I will make known my words unto you.
- Proverbs 1:23

If ye then, being evil, know how to give good gifts unto your children: how much more shall your heavenly Father give the Holy Spirit to them that ask him?
- Luke 11:13

And whatsoever ye shall ask in my name, that will I do, that the Father may be glorified in the Son.
- John 14:13

But ye shall receive power, after that the Holy Ghost is come upon you: and ye shall be witnesses unto me both in Jerusalem, and in all Judaea, and in Samaria, and unto the uttermost part of the earth.
- Acts 1:8

And it shall come to pass in the last days, saith God, I will pour out of my Spirit upon all flesh: and your sons and your daughters shall prophesy, and your young men shall see visions, and your old men shall dream dreams:
- Acts 2:17

Then Peter said unto them, Repent, and be baptized every one of you in the name of Jesus Christ for the remission of sins, and ye shall receive the gift of the Holy Ghost.
- Acts 2:38

That he would grant you, according to the riches of his glory, to be strengthened with might by his Spirit in the inner man; That Christ may dwell in your hearts by faith; that ye, being rooted and grounded in love, May be able to comprehend with all saints what is the breadth, and length, and depth, and height; And to know the love of Christ, which passeth knowledge, that ye might be filled with all the fulness of God. - Ephesians 3:16-19

Finances / Jobs

The LORD shall open unto thee his good treasure, the heaven to give the rain unto thy land in his season, and to bless all the work of thine hand: and thou shalt lend unto many nations, and thou shalt not borrow. - Deuteronomy 28:12

He becometh poor that dealeth with a slack hand: but the hand of the diligent maketh rich. - Proverbs 10:4

Wealth gotten by vanity shall be diminished: but he that gathereth by labour shall increase. - Proverbs 13:11

Bring ye all the tithes into the storehouse, that there may be meat in mine house, and prove me now herewith, saith the LORD of hosts, if I will not open you the windows of heaven, and pour you out a blessing, that there shall not be room enough to receive it. - Malachi 3:10

But seek ye first the kingdom of God, and his righteousness; and all these things shall be added unto you. - Matthew 6:33

But my God shall supply all your need according to his riches in glory by Christ Jesus. - Philippians 4:19

Forgiveness

If my people, which are called by my name, shall humble themselves, and pray, and seek my face, and turn from their wicked ways; then will I hear from heaven, and will forgive their sin, and will heal their land.
- 2 Chronicles 7:14

Thou hast forgiven the iniquity of thy people, thou hast covered all their sin. Selah.
- Psalms 85:2

For thou, Lord, art good, and ready to forgive; and plenteous in mercy unto all them that call upon thee.
- Psalms 86:5

And when ye stand praying, forgive, if ye have ought against any: that your Father also which is in heaven may forgive you your trespasses.
- Mark 11:25

And be ye kind one to another, tenderhearted, forgiving one another, even as God for Christ's sake hath forgiven you.
- Ephesians 4:32

If we confess our sins, he is faithful and just to forgive us our sins, and to cleanse us from all unrighteousness.
- 1 John 1:9

Guidance

And, behold, I am with thee, and will keep thee in all places whither thou goest, and will bring thee again into this land; for I will not leave thee, until I have done that which I have spoken to thee of.
- Genesis 28:15

Have not I commanded thee? Be strong and of a good courage; be not afraid, neither be thou dismayed: for the LORD thy God is with thee whithersoever thou goest.
- Joshua 1:9

What man is he that feareth the LORD? him shall he teach in the way that he shall choose.
- Psalms 25:12

I will instruct thee and teach thee in the way which thou shalt go: I will guide thee with mine eye.
- Psalms 32:8

Trust in the LORD with all thine heart; and lean not unto thine own understanding. In all thy ways acknowledge him, and he shall direct thy paths.
- Proverbs 3:5-6

And if thou draw out thy soul to the hungry, and satisfy the afflicted soul; then shall thy light rise in obscurity, and thy darkness be as the noon day:
- Isaiah 58:10

And it shall come to pass, that before they call, I will answer; and while they are yet speaking, I will hear.
- Isaiah 65:24

Call unto me, and I will answer thee, and shew thee great and mighty things, which thou knowest not.
- Jeremiah 33:3

Howbeit when he, the Spirit of truth, is come, he will guide you into all truth: for he shall not speak of himself; but whatsoever he shall hear, that shall he speak: and he will shew you things to come.
- John 16:13

If any of you lack wisdom, let him ask of God, that giveth to all men liberally, and upbraideth not; and it shall be given him.
- James 1:5

Health

And said, If thou wilt diligently hearken to the voice of the LORD thy God, and wilt do that which is right in his sight, and wilt give ear to his commandments, and keep all his statutes, I will put none of these diseases upon thee, which I have brought upon the Egyptians: for I am the LORD that healeth thee.
- Exodus 15:26

Bless the LORD, O my soul, and forget not all his benefits:
- Psalms 103:2

Be not wise in thine own eyes: fear the LORD, and depart from evil.
- Proverbs 3:7

But they that wait upon the LORD shall renew their strength; they shall mount up with wings as eagles; they shall run, and not be weary; and they shall walk, and not faint.
- Isaiah 40:31

But he was wounded for our transgressions, he was bruised for our iniquities: the chastisement of our peace was upon him; and with his stripes we are healed.
- Isaiah 53:5

Heal me, O LORD, and I shall be healed; save me, and I shall be saved: for thou art my praise.
- Jeremiah 17:14

For I will restore health unto thee, and I will heal thee of thy wounds, saith the LORD...
- Jeremiah 30:17

But unto you that fear my name shall the Sun of righteousness arise with healing in his wings; and ye shall go forth, and grow up as calves of the stall.
- Malachi 4:2

Is any sick among you? let him call for the elders of the church; and let them pray over him, anointing him with oil in the name of the Lord:
- James 5:14

Marriage / Companionship

And the LORD God said, It is not good that the man should be alone; I will make him an help meet for him.
- Genesis 2:18

Delight thyself also in the LORD: and he shall give thee the desires of thine heart.
- Psalms 37:4

God setteth the solitary in families...
- Psalms 68:6

Whoso findeth a wife findeth a good thing, and obtaineth favour of the LORD.
- Proverbs 18:22

For thy Maker is thine husband; the LORD of hosts is his name; and thy Redeemer the Holy One of Israel; The God of the whole earth shall he be called.
- Isaiah 54:5

For I know the thoughts that I think toward you, saith the LORD, thoughts of peace, and not of evil, to give you an expected end.
- Jeremiah 29:11

And this is the confidence that we have in him, that, if we ask any thing according to his will, he heareth us:
- 1 John 5:14

Salvation / God's Love

I have blotted out, as a thick cloud, thy transgressions, and, as a cloud, thy sins: return unto me; for I have redeemed thee.
- Isaiah 44:22

And I will deliver thee out of the hand of the wicked, and I will redeem thee out of the hand of the terrible.
- Jeremiah 15:21

For God so loved the world, that he gave his only begotten Son, that whosoever believeth in him should not perish, but have everlasting life.
- John 3:16

He that believeth on the Son hath everlasting life: and he that believeth not the Son shall not see life; but the wrath of God abideth on him.
- John 3:36

For the wages of sin is death; but the gift of God is eternal life through Jesus Christ our Lord.
- Romans 6:23

STOP, LISTEN & BREATH:

This section is designed for salient points and takes a ways from what you just read!

Notes:

_____

_____

_____

_____

_____

_____

_____

_____

_____

_____

_____

_____

_____

_____

_____

_____

_____

For I am persuaded, that neither death, nor life, nor angels, nor principalities, nor powers, nor things present, nor things to come, Nor height, nor depth, nor any other creature, shall be able to separate us from the love of God, which is in Christ Jesus our Lord.
- Romans 8:38-39

That if thou shalt confess with thy mouth the Lord Jesus, and shalt believe in thine heart that God hath raised him from the dead, thou shalt be saved. For with the heart man believeth unto righteousness; and with the mouth confession is made unto salvation.
- Romans 10:9-10

To the praise of the glory of his grace, wherein he hath made us accepted in the beloved. In whom we have redemption through his blood, the forgiveness of sins, according to the riches of his grace;
- Ephesians 1:6-7

Let your conversation be without covetousness; and be content with such things as ye have: for he hath said, I will never leave thee, nor forsake thee.
- Hebrews 13:5

He that overcometh, the same shall be clothed in white raiment; and I will not blot out his name out of the book of life, but I will confess his name before my Father, and before his angels.
- Revelation 3:5

Behold, I stand at the door, and knock: if any man hear my voice, and open the door, I will come in to him, and will sup with him, and he with me.
- Revelation 3:20

STOP, LISTEN & BREATH:

This section is designed for salient points and take a ways from what you just read!

    Notes:

_____

_____

_____

_____

_____

_____

_____

_____

_____

_____

_____

_____

_____

_____

_____

_____

_____

_____

Strength to do God's will

Wait on the LORD: be of good courage, and he shall strengthen thine heart: wait, I say, on the LORD.
- Psalms 27:14

He giveth power to the faint; and to them that have no might he increaseth strength.
- Isaiah 40:29

No weapon that is formed against thee shall prosper; and every tongue that shall rise against thee in judgment thou shalt condemn. This is the heritage of the servants of the LORD, and their righteousness is of me, saith the LORD.
- Isaiah 54:17

A new heart also will I give you, and a new spirit will I put within you: and I will take away the stony heart out of your flesh, and I will give you an heart of flesh.

- Ezekiel 36:26

For our light affliction, which is but for a moment, worketh for us a far more exceeding and eternal weight of glory;
- 2 Corinthians 4:17

And let us not be weary in well doing: for in due season we shall reap, if we faint not.
- Galatians 6:9

Being confident of this very thing, that he which hath begun a good work in you will perform it until the day of Jesus Christ:
- Philippians 1:6

I can do all things through Christ which strengtheneth me.
- Philippians 4:13
> NIV > 1 Samuel 2
◀ 1 Samuel 2 ▶
New International Version
Hannah's Prayer

<u>1</u>Then Hannah prayed and said:
"My heart rejoices in the Lord;
in the Lord my horn*a* is lifted high.
My mouth boasts over my enemies,
for I delight in your deliverance.
<u>2</u>"There is no one holy like the Lord;
there is no one besides you;
there is no Rock like our God.
<u>3</u>"Do not keep talking so proudly
or let your mouth speak such arrogance,
for the Lord is a God who knows,
and by him deeds are weighed.
<u>4</u>"The bows of the warriors are broken,
but those who stumbled are armed with strength.
<u>5</u>Those who were full hire themselves out for food,
but those who were hungry are hungry no more.

She who was barren has borne seven children,
but she who has had many sons pines away.
6"The Lord brings death and makes alive;
he brings down to the grave and raises up.
7The Lord sends poverty and wealth;
he humbles and he exalts.
8He raises the poor from the dust
and lifts the needy from the ash heap;
he seats them with princes
and has them inherit a throne of honor.
"For the foundations of the earth are the Lord's;
on them he has set the world.
9He will guard the feet of his faithful servants,
but the wicked will be silenced in the place of darkness.
"It is not by strength that one prevails;
10those who oppose the Lord will be broken.
The Most High will thunder from heaven;
the Lord will judge the ends of the earth.
"He will give strength to his king
and exalt the horn of his anointed."
11Then Elkanah went home to Ramah, but the boy
ministered before the Lord under Eli the priest.

STOP, LISTEN & BREATH:

This section is designed for salient points and takes a ways from what you just read!

Eli's Wicked Sons

12Eli's sons were scoundrels; they had no regard for the Lord. **13**Now it was the practice of the priests that, whenever any of the people offered a sacrifice, the priest's servant would come with a three-pronged fork in his hand while the meat was being boiled **14**and would plunge the fork into the pan or kettle or caldron or pot. Whatever the fork brought up the priest would take for himself. This is how they treated all the

Israelites who came to Shiloh. **15**But even before the fat was burned, the priest's servant would come and say to the person who was sacrificing, "Give the priest some meat to roast; he won't accept boiled meat from you, but only raw."

16If the person said to him, "Let the fat be burned first, and then take whatever you want," the servant would answer, "No, hand it over now; if you don't, I'll take it by force."

17This sin of the young men was very great in the Lord's sight, for they*b* were treating the Lord's offering with contempt.

18But Samuel was ministering before the Lord—a boy wearing a linen ephod. **19**Each year his mother made him a little robe and took it to him when she went up with her husband to offer the annual sacrifice.**20**Eli would bless Elkanah and his wife, saying, "May the Lord give you children by this woman to take the place of the one she prayed for and gave to*c* the Lord." Then they would go home. **21**And the Lord was gracious to Hannah; she gave birth to three sons and two daughters. Meanwhile, the boy Samuel grew up in the presence of the Lord.

22Now Eli, who was very old, heard about everything his sons were doing to all Israel and how they slept with the women who served at the entrance to the tent of meeting. **23**So he said to them, "Why do you do such things? I hear from all the people about these wicked deeds of yours. **24**No, my sons; the report I hear spreading among the Lord's people is not good. **25**If one person sins against another, God may mediate for the offender; but if anyone sins against the Lord, who will intercede for them?" His sons, however, did not listen to their father's rebuke, for it was the Lord's will to put them to death.

26And the boy Samuel continued to grow in stature and in favor with the Lord and with people.

STOP, LISTEN & BREATH:

This section is designed for salient points and take a ways from what you just read!

    Notes:

_____

_____

_____

_____

_____

_____

_____

_____

_____

_____

_____

_____

_____

_____

_____

_____

Prophecy Against the House of Eli

27Now a man of God came to Eli and said to him, "This is what the Lord says: 'Did I not clearly reveal myself to your ancestor's family when they were in Egypt under Pharaoh? **28**I chose your ancestor out of all the tribes of Israel to be my priest, to go up to my altar, to burn incense, and to wear an ephod in my presence. I also gave your ancestor's family all the food offerings presented by the Israelites. **29**Why do you*e* scorn my sacrifice and offering that I prescribed for my dwelling? Why do you honor your sons more than me by fattening yourselves on the choice parts of every offering made by my people Israel?'

30"Therefore the Lord, the God of Israel, declares: 'I promised that members of your family would minister before me forever.' But now the Lord declares: 'Far be it from me! Those who honor me I will honor, but those who despise me will be disdained. **31**The time is coming when I will cut short your strength and the strength of your priestly house, so that no one in it will reach old age, **32**and you will see distress in my dwelling. Although good will be done to Israel, no one in your family line will ever reach old age. **33**Every one of you that I do not cut off from serving at my altar I will spare only to destroy your sight and sap your strength, and all your descendants will die in the prime of life.

34" 'And what happens to your two sons, Hophni and Phinehas, will be a sign to you—they will both die on the same day. **35**I will raise up for myself a faithful priest, who will do according to what is in my heart and mind. I will firmly establish his priestly house, and they will minister before my anointed one always. **36**Then everyone left in your family line will come and bow down before him for a piece of silver and a loaf of bread and plead, "Appoint me to some priestly office so I can have food to eat." ""

STOP, LISTEN & BREATH:

This section is designed for salient points and takes a ways from what you just read!

Notes:

_____

_____

_____

_____

_____

_____

_____

_____

_____

_____

_____

Chapter 19

Knowing Your True Value

One of the essential components of being a Christian is to understand you are no longer your own person. This means that you have been adopted into a royal family. A royal priesthood, a family no longer made by man. Yes you had a physical birth by man but know you have been allowed to be a part of God's plan for your life. God has created a plan that will secure our destiny here on earth and eternity.

The eternal part is often misunderstood by Christians, because we don't get a true picture of eternal life while here on earth therefore it becomes a challenge. Especially when are challenged by the tricks and dangerous pitfalls of the enemy. The awesome thing is that God's word defeats the enemy every time we activate it. The scriptures tell us that God's people perish because of ignorance (lack of knowledge). Simply, we must understand how to skillfully activate God's word for ourselves. When we do this, the Bible says the enemy will flee. God loves us so much more than we can phantom.

Why does God Loves us so?

Ephesians 2:10New International Version (NIV)
10 For we are God's handiwork, created in Christ Jesus to do good works, which God prepared in advance for us to do.

God loved us despite what we may think of ourselves. God sees in us something for greater than we see in ourselves. Despite your past or even current dynamic or what others think of us. Once we are fully connected to God he cleaned us from our past reproach.

Joshua 5:9
LORD said to Joshua, "Today I have rolled away the reproach of Egypt from you." So the place has been called Gilgal to this day override for those who grieve in Zion--

Isaiah 61:3
to bestow on them a crown of beauty instead of ashes, the oil of joy instead of mourning, and a garment of praise instead of a spirit of despair. They will be called oaks of righteousness, a planting of the LORD for the display of his splendor.

What would the World be like without the Holy Spirit?

God's hands is a sifter and only what he allows to come through can get to you so if he allowed it to come through it is for you Nothing can come through unless he allows it

Isaiah 49:14-16
We have often looked for the hand of God and we can't seem to feel it or see it. However God is always there working on my behalf

Motivational Moment

God never slumber nor does he sleep

Sometimes we find ourselves in a dark place where we pray and pray and it seems like God has forgotten about us and it seems as if God has not moved and I'm running out of time but God does not work on our time. While you're waiting and it seems as if nothing is going but God is building a fortress in us. Some of us wouldn't praise him without going through trials but God says I have you in my hands and no man can pluck you out of my hands. We have to learn to train our spirit so that when we don't see or feel God is doing anything but he is busy doing the work. God is still at work and he has the answer to your dilemma even though you can't see him, you can't see him because he is working on your behalf he will take the very thing you have and turn it around because he specialized in doing the impossible. Don't count it a loss because you are going through, it's because of the going through you can get to God.

God is right there in the midst of what you are going through and by all means don't lose the joy while on the journey

Ephesians 6:11-18King James Version (KJV)

11 Put on the whole armour of God, that ye may be able to stand against the wiles of the devil.
12 For we wrestle not against flesh and blood, but against principalities, against powers, against the rulers of the darkness of this world, against spiritual wickedness in high places.
13 Wherefore take unto you the whole armour of God, that ye may be able to withstand in the evil day, and having done all, to stand.
14 Stand therefore, having your loins girt about with truth, and having on the breastplate of righteousness;
15 And your feet shod with the preparation of the gospel of peace;
16 Above all, taking the shield of faith, wherewith ye shall be able to quench all the fiery darts of the wicked.
17 And take the helmet of salvation, and the sword of the Spirit, which is the word of God:
18 Praying always with all prayer and supplication in the Spirit, and watching thereunto with all perseverance and supplication for all saints;
King James Version (KJV)
Public Domain

Satan tactics is to put pressure on us to take our mind so he can control your mind and your thought. Believers often fail to make quick decisions when one is ignored to Satan's devise. God's remedies for Vic the believer must know his weapons.

Satan is the head of his kingdom ruling spirit make sure when we are in prayer that we kill off the strong man aka Satan!

Daniel chapter 10 Satan holds of the angel of the Lord. Black men are being killed off both old and young

Nothing worse than a tormented soul

Luke 10: the power to walk in Gods spirit

Mark16:17 casting out devils the power given the believer God has already given us all the power to overcome the enemy we recognize Satan as a defeated fold. Jesus declares that Satan has no power.

Evil power only has one objective and that's evil. There is no advantage to ignore Satan. God is raising up a powerful army.

References:

The following information sources were used to prepare and update the above essay. The hyperlinks are not necessarily still active today.

1. Reb Gershon Caudill, *"A Heterosexual Jewish Rebbe's View on the (Supposedly) Homosexual Texts in the Hebrew Bible,"* at: http://www.affirmation.org/
2. "Elaine," "Sodom and Gomorrah," Gay Church, at: http://www.gaychurch.org/
3. Father Basil Isaacs, *"Proofx booklet"*, *Fountain of Life Western Orthodox Church* Catholic Mission
4. We refer to *"the author of Jude"* rather than use his name. This is because there is no consensus on the identity of the author. Conservative Christian theologians generally believe that the book was written by Jude, a brother of Jesus circa 67 to 73 CE. Liberal theologians generally believe that the author is unknown, and that the book was written sometime within that era.

Printed in the United States
By Bookmasters

Printed in the United States
By Bookmasters